For my queen Sascha, my beautiful princess
Claudia and my little warrior Morgan. You are my
everything, the people I look up to, the ones I look
forward to, the best of me, my biggest treasures.

With love y cariño,
King Papa

# FEAST

## 100 GENEROUS RECIPES TO SHARE

### MIGUEL MAESTRE

plum. Pan Macmillan Australia

# CONTENTS

INTRODUCTION 7

THE SPANISH KITCHEN 12

BRUNCH 17

SALADS & VEGETABLES 41

PASTA & RICE 69

PIES 91

FISH & SEAFOOD 107

CHICKEN 135

MEAT 153

PIZZA & BREAD 177

DESSERTS 189

CAKES & BISCUITS 207

CHRISTMAS 231

GRACIAS 256

INDEX 259

# INTRODUCTION

I arrived in Australia with broken English, an empty wallet and a suitcase full of dreams. I have since made this country my home and it is where my career as a chef has really taken flight.

From the first day I set foot in a commercial kitchen, I felt like I was on a great journey of discovery. If I'm honest, it is the only place I've ever felt I truly belonged. I am an extremely hyperactive person and I have always found it hard to focus in other settings, so I was very lucky to find my place through cooking. I had previously worked in a shop, in sales and marketing and in various other roles, but in the kitchen, for the first time, I felt like I could channel all my energy into a job. Rather than being a negative thing – my legs twitching under the desk at the office! – my energy levels saw me excel. While chefs younger than me would be broken by the end of a busy service, I would still be standing and ready to go. Finally, it felt like a positive thing to be doing lots of different things at the same time, and the physicality of the job was perfect for me. The kitchen felt like where I was meant to be and I fell in love with food.

I began my cooking career in Edinburgh at the age of 18. I had finished school back home in Spain, tried my hand at a few other jobs like helping my mum in her shop, but ultimately wanted to head overseas on an adventure. It was while working in a restaurant in Edinburgh that I met my future wife, Sascha, who was a waitress there at the time. When I finished my chef's apprenticeship at 21, Sascha and I decided to give her hometown of Sydney, Australia, a try. I loved it straight away and, as you can see, we never left!

I started right back at the bottom in Sydney restaurants; I never took for granted the opportunities I was given, eventually working alongside some of the country's best chefs. I probably learned the most from Tony Bilson, one of the true founding fathers of Australian cuisine. Tony gave me a solid foundation in the French classics – jus, confit, partridge, bouillabaisse – and taught me the importance of hard work and dedication to my craft. It was like being at the best cooking school in the world, working alongside Tony and his team.

Another highlight was meeting Ferran Adrià and being invited by him to cook at his famed Spanish restaurant, El Bulli. This was the other end of the spectrum to cooking with Tony, as it was all about innovation, modernity and really pushing the boundaries of food. The old-school techniques I learned with Tony, coupled with the new-school innovation at El Bulli, put me on the path to becoming the chef I am today.

My cooking really blossomed in Australia, with the amazing and abundant fresh produce we have here. My Spanish style of cooking is all about generosity, big flavours and shared feasting, and I found these things translated perfectly to Australian palates. Australians are great travellers and always keen to embrace new flavours and ideas, so I have found touring the country with food and wine festivals and other events over the years to be incredibly rewarding.

At 28, I opened my own Spanish restaurant: El Toro Loco (The Crazy Bull), named for the totem animal of Spain. I wanted it to be like my personality in restaurant form: full-on, passionate and intense! El Toro Loco was so loud, with its open kitchen, flamenco dancers, trumpeter and bell ringing at the pass. It was more of an experience or performance than just a dinner out. The open kitchen was raised on a platform – the first thing you saw as you entered the restaurant – and I was on show there every day. This was how I really became well known (and how I picked up the nickname, El Toro Loco).

My restaurant and my work in high-profile events soon led me to the world of television, working on shows such as *Boys Weekend*, *Miguel's Tropical Kitchen*, *Miguel's Feast* and *The Living Room*. At the same time, Sascha and I were growing our little family. The things I'm proudest of in life are being a husband to Sascha, father to Claudia and Morgan, and son to Antonio Luis and Florentina. These are the people I look up to; they mean everything to me.

My second family is the one I've found through *The Living Room*: Gringo, Bazz and Amanda. Working with them is more of a lifestyle than a job, and the success of the show is really due to our friendship. Some of my most beautiful memories are of travelling with them all around Australia and the world and being welcomed into Australian living rooms every Friday night. *The Living Room* has given me so many opportunities to cook with amazing Australian ingredients and meet almost every farmer and producer in this incredible country – not to mention cooking alongside some of the world's best chefs. These experiences have really shaped my cooking style into what it is today: versatile, multicultural, achievable and fun.

Although Australia is now my home, I remain a proud ambassador for Spanish food. A few years ago I was presented the Order of Civil Merits by His Majesty King Felipe VI, King of Spain – the highest and most prestigious award a Spanish citizen can receive. Only three other chefs in Spanish history have received this award, and it was my proudest moment as a chef and entertainer. Not far behind that was being crowned King of the Jungle in the reality show *I'm a Celebrity … Get Me Out of Here!* This experience was something that really tested and changed me as a person. It made me value the importance of family above all.

As you flip through this book, you'll come to understand my cooking style. To me, life is a feast for the senses and all meals should be generous, unique, fun, original and colourful. I am always looking for ways of doing things differently … some might say I get a little crazy (like using a PVC pipe to make pumpketta, see page 58). After all, as the great Anthony Bourdain once said, 'your body is not a temple, it's an amusement park'.

This book has something for everyone: quick and delicious meals like my best-ever jaffles (page 22); fresh bites for healthy eaters like the Murcian salad (page 43) or zoodles (page 50); an outstanding tomahawk steak to please any carnivore (page 166); hot smoked salmon (page 132), crispy barramundi (page 126) or lobster caldero (page 77) to keep the seafood connoisseurs happy; and the most delicious desserts, from Aussie classics to traditional Spanish sweets. I've even included a Christmas chapter, with plenty of inspiration to achieve that wow factor centrepiece with minimum effort.

There is truly a dish for every meal in here, from a quick brunch to a romantic dinner, a weeknight paella to a weekend project like making curry from scratch. There are very simple recipes and ones to challenge kneadier cooks (such as different types of pastries), as well as favourites from family and friends, like Claudia's crepes (page 30) or Amanda Keller's jam drops (page 221). Instagrammers chasing lots of likes need to try the ice cream cake on page 215! It's a true masterpiece (or Maestrepiece?).

This is my repertoire, from my kitchen and my heart to yours. Love is the best ingredient in life – it makes everything taste better.

Chop chop,

*Miguel*
xx

# THE SPANISH KITCHEN

## ANCHOVIES

Spanish anchovies really take your cooking to the next level. They are not as salty as other varieties, and used in salads and dressings they are amazing! You will see plenty of white anchovies used in this book. Known as boquerones, they are pickled in vinegar, and once you taste them you'll never use another anchovy again. In Spain, we eat these on bread with pickles as a snack. Yum!

## CHORIZO

The most famous sausage in the world, without a doubt! Made with pork and delicious spices, the most dominant flavour is paprika – this is where the rich, red colour comes from. Chorizo is a versatile ingredient that works with every cuisine, technique and meal – it's my ultimate favourite. The best chorizo is made with free-range pork.

## EXTRA-VIRGIN OLIVE OIL

In Australia, we have the best and freshest extra-virgin olive oil from different regions throughout the country. This is an absolutely essential ingredient in the Mediterranean diet, with amazing health benefits.

## JAMON

The king of hams. Salty and delicate, jamon is a Spanish dried ham with amazing seasoning power when combined with other ingredients. I love to eat it fresh as part of a charcuterie board, in a sandwich (see my jaffles on page 22) or as part of a fine-dining meal.

## MANCHEGO

This is the preferred cheese in Spain, with the best-quality varieties produced in La Mancha. Manchego is made with sheep's milk and has a lovely nutty flavour. It is widely available at supermarkets throughout Australia and makes a great alternative to parmesan in your cooking. If you wish to grate it, use the aged variety; it you want to melt it, use a fresher one.

## PAELLA PAN

The secret to cooking a perfect paella is having the right pan. If you want to cook this dish like a pro, it is well worth investing in one, as they are designed to evaporate the stock correctly and create the perfect caramelised crust on the bottom (known as soccarrada; every member of a Spanish family fights for this as it has the ultimate umami flavour!). Paella pans look fantastic as a centrepiece on the table – perfect for families enjoying this great sharing dish.

## PAPRIKA

Paprika is the most well-known Spanish ingredient in Australia. It has three different flavour profiles: sweet, smoky and spicy. This means you can choose your favourite flavour for dry rubs, marinades and adding to pretty much any dish you like. I recommend using Spanish paprika if you can, as it's of the highest quality. Once opened, store it in the fridge to keep moist. My favourite brand is Red Gold (Oro Rojo). This particular paprika comes from my home town of Murcia, so maybe I'm a little bit biased!

## PIQUILLO PEPPERS

These small, sweet chillies are traditionally grown in northern Spain, and are a great way to add a bit of zing to salads or sauces. They are roasted and sold in jars at most major supermarkets.

## ROMESCO

This is a very famous Spanish sauce, with a roasted capsicum and almond base. It will take your grilled meats to the next level. For a recipe, see page 174.

## SAFFRON

Saffron is one of the main flavours in Spanish cuisine. It is a unique ingredient that is very expensive because of the way it's harvested. A saffron flower has only three stems and these three stems are hand-picked, so to get a kilo of saffron, you would require between 80,000 and 180,000 flowers depending on the size of the stem. Imagine how lucky you'd be if your partner bought you so many flowers! I recommend using saffron fresh. A lot of recipes say to toast it, but it is easily burnt. To get the most colour out of the saffron, you need to soak it in water for at least an hour prior to use.

## SOFRITO

This classic flavour base is the soul of every great Spanish dish. The main ingredient is tomato, which is combined with garlic, herbs and olive oil. It can be made by hand or in a food processor for ease, and keeps very well in the fridge or freezer. It's great to have on hand to add to veggies, meats, fish, rice or pasta dishes. For a recipe, see page 70 or page 82.

## SPANISH BOMBA RICE

If you want to cook the perfect paella or Spanish rice dish, this is the only variety to use. Widely available in delis throughout Australia, it is a short-grain rice with a pearly white colour. The most important quality of Spanish rice is its ability to absorb three times its volume in water or stock without splitting or overcooking. You can cook it over high heat for the entire cooking process and it will always give the perfect crust (soccarrada) to your paella. People often ask me if they can use arborio rice for paella and I tell them, you don't use two-minute noodles to cook fettuccine! Using the right rice is essential for Spanish cooking. The best-quality Spanish rice comes in a fabric bag. My favourite variety is Calasparra.

# BRUNCH

# CORN & ZUCCHINI FRITTERS

## WITH HALOUMI

These yummy and healthy corn and zucchini fritters can be cooked up for breakfast, lunch or dinner. They are also a great option for a veggie burger. I like to serve them with tomato chutney – they're delicious with a poached egg, too.

The trick to these is to spiralise or julienne the zucchini rather than grate it, for maximum flavour and minimal oxidisation. Also, be sure to grate the corn kernels rather than using them whole – it intensifies the corn flavour and makes the fritters easier to eat.

225 g (1 ½ cups) self-raising flour
50 g (½ cup) finely grated
   parmesan or manchego
salt flakes and freshly ground
   black pepper
½ bunch of chives, roughly chopped
250 ml (1 cup) milk, plus extra
   if needed
2 eggs
2 corn cobs, husks and
   silks removed
olive oil, for pan-frying
2 zucchini, spiralised or julienned
180 g block of haloumi,
   thickly sliced
chutney or relish, baby rocket
   leaves and lemon wedges,
   to serve

**SERVES 4**

Place the flour and parmesan or manchego in a large bowl, season with salt and pepper and mix well with clean hands. Add the chives.

Whisk together the milk and eggs in a small bowl, then gradually pour into the flour mixture, whisking constantly to make a thick batter the consistency of creamy mash. Add a little extra milk if needed.

Grate the corn using a box grater to separate the flesh from the cob. Add to the batter and mix well.

Heat a splash of oil in a frying pan over medium heat. Working in batches, lower a small handful of zucchini strips into the batter to coat. Lift it out of the batter with two spoons, place in the frying pan and cook for 2–3 minutes until golden on the base, then turn and cook for another 1–2 minutes until cooked through. Remove and drain on paper towel. Repeat with the remaining zucchini and batter to make 12 fritters all up.

Add the haloumi slices to the pan and cook for about 30 seconds each side or until golden.

Spoon some chutney or relish onto each plate, then layer with one fritter, some rocket, two slices of haloumi, and top with another couple of fritters. Serve with lemon wedges and extra chutney or relish on the side.

# BEETROOT, ZUCCHINI & TOMATO GALETTE

## WITH AMAZING BUTTERY PASTRY

One of the scariest things for home cooks is making pastry from scratch. Well, don't stress anymore as my rough puff will make you feel like a pastry master with minimum effort and massive returns! The secret is to use your fingers to crumble the butter with the flour, making sure it stays coarse so that little pillows of buttery flavour will make the pastry delicious. You can forget about lining a tart case as this is a very rustic way to contain the filling, and feel free to be inventive with how you pinch the edges. Just be aware that whatever shape you make will sink slightly and this is fine. For the filling, whatever veggies are in season will do. I promise you that this recipe will became a family favourite.

1 beetroot, cut into 2 mm
  thick slices
1 small red onion, finely sliced
  into rounds
1 small zucchini, cut into 2 mm
  thick slices
2 rainbow chard stalks, ribs and
  stems removed, leaves torn into
  bite-sized pieces (or use English
  spinach or Tuscan kale)
1 tablespoon extra-virgin olive oil
1 teaspoon thyme leaves
salt flakes and freshly ground
  black pepper
200 g truss cherry tomatoes
  on the vine
1 egg, lightly beaten

**ROUGH PUFF PASTRY**
200 g (1⅓ cups) plain flour,
  plus extra for dusting
½ teaspoon salt flakes
200 g chilled unsalted butter,
  cut into small cubes
½ tablespoon chilled water

**FILLING**
200 g fresh full-cream ricotta,
  well drained
100 g soft Persian feta
1 tablespoon finely chopped chives
salt flakes and freshly ground
  black pepper

**SERVES 6-8**

To make the pastry, combine the flour and salt in a bowl. Add the butter and rub in with your fingertips until the mixture resembles coarse breadcrumbs. Gradually add the water and mix until the dough begins to form a ball. Turn out onto a lightly floured bench and knead briefly to bring the dough together.

Place the dough on a sheet of baking paper, dusted with extra flour, and roll out to a 32 cm round, about 3 mm thick. Using the paper, transfer the dough to a baking tray and refrigerate for 20–30 minutes.

Meanwhile, to make the filling, place the ricotta, feta and chives in a bowl and mix well with a fork. Season with salt and pepper.

Preheat the oven to 220°C (fan-forced).

Meanwhile, place the beetroot, onion, zucchini, chard, oil and thyme leaves in a bowl, season to taste and toss to combine.

Take the dough out of the fridge and spread evenly with the ricotta filling, leaving a 3 cm border.

Arrange the beetroot rounds around the edge, then pile the greens in the middle (the beetroot will hold the rest in place). Fold the edge of the pastry up and over the filling, leaving the centre exposed. Place the tomatoes in the centre.

Lightly brush the dough with egg wash, then bake for 25–30 minutes until the pastry is golden and the vegetables are tender. Remove and leave the galette to cool slightly on the tray. Serve warm or at room temperature.

# JAMON & MANCHEGO JAFFLES

I'm always looking for different ways to maximise the texture and flavour of ingredients in my cooking. I've never seen anyone make jaffles this way before and that's why I'm extremely proud of this recipe, my signature jaffle. The jamon wrapped around the outside becomes crispy, while the cheese inside melts and the grated tomato becomes juicy and fresh. Just don't eat it straight away as that tomato will be a million degrees and will burn your tongue.

Jamon is such a rewarding ingredient. In Spain, there are shops that only sell jamon; it is quite mesmerising to see the butcher slicing it straight from the leg. Eat it by itself, or paired with manchego it is seriously one of my favourite flavour combinations. Your ham and cheese sangas will never be the same again!

butter, for spreading
4 slices of white bread
2 ripe truss tomatoes
2 small garlic cloves, finely grated
1 tablespoon extra-virgin olive oil
salt flakes and freshly ground
    black pepper
150 g (1½ cups) grated manchego
6 thin slices of jamon
6 sage leaves

**SERVES 2**

Lightly butter the bread on both sides and get your sandwich press heating.

Grate the tomato into a large bowl, discarding the peel. Stir in the garlic and oil and season well with salt and pepper.

Spread half the grated cheese over one slice of bread. Top with half the garlicky tomato mixture and sandwich with another slice of bread. Repeat for the second sandwich.

Wrap three slices of the jamon around each sandwich and arrange the sage leaves on top. Place in the sandwich press and cook for 5 minutes or until the sage leaves and jamon are crisp and the cheese has melted.

Leave to cool for 5 minutes before eating – that hot tomato can be lethal!

# OKONOMIYAKI WITH CHIMICHURRI

Japanese cuisine is one of my top five favourites: it's dynamic, colourful, intense, fresh and, most importantly, fun.

I first discovered okonomiyaki at our local markets in Narrabeen, and I think it is one of the greatest pancakes in culinary history. The Japanese stall holder cooks these massive pancakes and serves them with kewpie, sriracha, sesame and chipotle mayo.

This dish combines cabbage (very healthy) and every Australian's favourite cooking device, the barbecue. Okonomiyaki can be eaten for any meal of the day, but it's a great go-to for brunch. You can make one big pancake and cut it into pizza slices, or make little ones to serve individually.

It's very hard to overcook or undercook an okonomiyaki; this is a bulletproof recipe. It's also very versatile. You can add chorizo or be adventurous and use grilled fish, prawns or poached eggs for brekkie.

80 g plain flour
2 eggs
200 g (2⅔ cups) shredded cabbage
3 spring onions, green parts only,
   finely sliced
1 chorizo sausage, finely sliced
   on the diagonal
2 tablespoons crumbled Greek feta
   (optional)
your choice of coriander leaves,
   shichimi togarashi, furikake and
   Japanese mayonnaise (kewpie),
   to serve

**CHIMICHURRI**
2 garlic cloves, finely chopped
1 long red chilli, deseeded and
   finely chopped
juice of ½ lemon
small handful of flat-leaf
   parsley leaves
small handful of coriander leaves
80 ml (⅓ cup) extra-virgin olive oil
salt flakes and freshly ground
   black pepper

**SERVES 2**

To make the chimichurri, place all the ingredients in a blender and blitz to your preferred consistency. Taste and adjust the seasoning if necessary.

Mix together the flour, eggs and 100 ml of water in a bowl to form a smooth batter. Fold in the cabbage and spring onion.

Heat a medium frying pan or barbecue hot plate over high heat. Add the batter and use a scraper to shape it into a circle about 20 cm in diameter. Cook for 5 minutes, allowing the water and cabbage to steam and a crust to form on the bottom. Flip the pancake over and cook for another 5 minutes.

At the same time, cook the chorizo slices in the pan or on the hot plate until crispy. Dress in 1 tablespoon of the chimichurri.

Slide the pancake onto a plate and top with the crispy chorizo and feta, if using. Drizzle with 2 tablespoons of chimichurri and serve hot, topped with your choice of toppings. Store any leftover chimichurri in an airtight container in the fridge for up to 2 weeks.

Jamon & Manchego Jaffles, see page 22
Flamenca Eggs, see page 28
Five-minute Tortilla de Patatas, see page 29

# FLAMENCA EGGS

As a nation of travellers, it's no surprise Australians are in love with international brekkie styles. Huevos rancheros, eggs benedict, French omelette, shakshuka … the list is never-ending.

One dish that we don't often see on cafe menus is the Spanish classic flamenca eggs, a baked egg and tomato dish which in my opinion is one of the healthiest and most nourishing breakfasts around. Flamenca eggs are great made with the amazing tomatoes that we have here in Australia. You can turn up the heat a little to make it more spicy and cook the eggs to your liking, but there is something special about the runny centre of the poached egg. When you poach eggs in tomato, the freshness of the tomato infuses the egg whites and the flavour is so refreshing.

This is a great Spanish way to start the day and goes beautifully with cured meats, such as jamon, salchichón and chorizo.

4 large oxheart tomatoes
  (the size of your fist)
1 tablespoon olive oil
1 long red chilli, halved, deseeded
  and chopped
2 garlic cloves, finely chopped
300 ml tomato juice
salt flakes and freshly ground
  black pepper
4 eggs
2 tablespoons grated manchego
2 slices of jamon, torn (optional)
sourdough bread and marinated
  feta, to serve

## TOMATO SALAD
250 g yellow mini heirloom
  tomatoes, halved
¼ bunch of mint, leaves picked
¼ bunch of basil, leaves picked
1 tablespoon extra-virgin olive oil
salt flakes and freshly ground
  black pepper

**SERVES 4**

Preheat the oven to 180°C (fan-forced). Line a baking tray with baking paper.

To make the tomato salad, combine all the ingredients in a large bowl. Set aside.

Cut the tops off the oxheart tomatoes and reserve, then slice a little off the bottom to give them a stable base. Scoop out the pulp and seeds (save them and add them to the tomato salad). Place the tomato shells on the prepared baking tray.

Heat the oil in a medium saucepan over medium heat, add the chilli and garlic and cook for 1 minute until softened. Stir in the tomato juice and cook, stirring, for another 5 minutes or until thickened. Season to taste. Carefully crack the eggs into the sauce and poach for 1 minute.

Spoon the hot tomato mixture into the prepared shells. Don't fill them right to the top – you want to leave room for the eggs. Use a ladle to carefully transfer the eggs without breaking the yolks, then sprinkle with some of the cheese.

Bake for about 5 minutes or until the tomato shells are tender and the egg whites are set, but the yolks are still a little runny (or cooked to your liking). Remove from the oven and sprinkle with the jamon, if using, and the remaining cheese.

Arrange the salad on serving plates and top with the baked tomatoes. Serve with sourdough spread with marinated feta for dipping into the tomatoes.

*Pictured on page 27.*

# FIVE-MINUTE TORTILLA DE PATATAS

This recipe was invented by the greatest chef in the world, Ferran Adrià from El Bulli. I met Ferran when he was visiting Australia and he was fascinated by how a young chef from Murcia could have his own TV show here. He invited me to cook with him for a few days at El Bulli in Spain. Considering the waitlist to work for free at his restaurant was three years, it was the opportunity of a lifetime!

Ferran is always looking for different ways to cook simple ingredients, and this is a great example. With just a few eggs and your favourite packet of chips, you can create a Spanish classic in a matter of minutes. Everyone should give this a go!

4 eggs
150 g thick, plain potato chips (or experiment with other flavours!), lightly crushed
salt flakes and freshly ground black pepper
2 teaspoons olive oil
1 teaspoon chopped flat-leaf parsley leaves
green salad, to serve

**MY QUICK AIOLI**
1 egg, straight from the fridge
5 drops of lemon juice
1 garlic clove, finely chopped
pinch of salt flakes
250 ml (1 cup) light olive oil

**SERVES 2**

To make the aioli, crack the egg into the beaker of a stick blender and add the remaining ingredients. Insert the stick blender, making sure it goes all the way to the bottom of the beaker, and blend until emulsified. Gradually move the blender up the beaker until your aioli is a nice creamy consistency.

Lightly whisk the eggs in a bowl to break up the yolks. Add the crushed chips and season with a little salt and pepper.

Heat the oil in a small frying pan over medium heat. Add the egg mixture and cook for about 3 minutes until just set.

Invert the tortilla onto a plate, then slide it back into the pan and cook for another 2 minutes.

Top with chopped parsley and serve with salad and aioli.

*Pictured on page 26.*

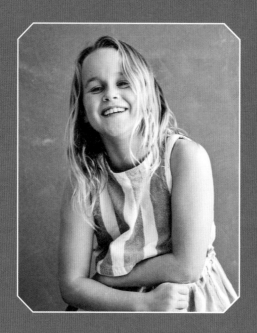

# CLAUDIA'S CINNAMON CREPES

Claudia is the most successful, charming and best-looking Maestre. She's our princess.

We're real early birds in our house and Claudia loves her breakfast. She's always been fascinated by flipping pancakes, and crepes are the safest way to do this because they don't break easily and are very thin.

Claudia has also loved the flavour of cinnamon since she was very little. I cooked these crepes with her on TV when she was very small and she stole the show. She's made them many times since.

This is the perfect recipe to get your kids involved with; just add some berries and banana to serve. I hope this becomes your family favourite, too.

300 g (2 cups) plain flour
115 g (½ cup) caster sugar
pinch of ground cinnamon
2 eggs
375 ml (1½ cups) milk, plus extra
   if needed
light olive oil, for pan-frying
butter, for pan-frying
sliced banana and strawberries,
   to serve
maple syrup, to serve

**SERVES 4**

Combine the flour, sugar and cinnamon in a large bowl. Add the eggs and milk and whisk to form a smooth batter, adding a little extra milk if needed.

Heat a little oil and a teaspoon of butter in a frying pan over medium heat. Add a ladleful of batter and tilt the pan to spread it out evenly and cover the base. Cook for 3–4 minutes or until bubbles appear, then carefully flip it over and cook another 2–3 minutes until golden and cooked through. Remove. Repeat with the remaining batter to make 10 to 12 crepes all up, adding more oil and butter as needed.

Stack the crepes, top with sliced banana and strawberries, and drizzle with maple syrup.

# POSH CHICKEN, HERB & MAYO
## FINGER SANDWICHES

These are the poshest chicken sandwiches in the universe. We made them for the Melbourne Grand Prix a few years ago, when I was executive chef. I was in charge of dining in the marquees and we needed to think of a fancy sandwich to serve, with the help of a local catering company. We made about 3000 of these.

The secret to these sandwiches is to use a silky mayo, soft white bread and an old-school electric knife with a serrated attachment. This knife is a game changer because it means there's no pressure on the soft bread when you slice it!

Don't skip the step of peeling the celery; when it's peeled it's like biting into cold water and elevates the sandwich even more. You can also add extra ingredients to make these sandwiches your own.

½ barbecue chicken, bones removed
45 g (½ cup) flaked almonds, toasted
1 small celery stick, peeled and finely chopped
finely grated zest of 1 lemon
160 g (⅔ cup) Japanese mayonnaise (kewpie)
½ bunch of chives, finely chopped
handful of flat-leaf parsley leaves, chopped
handful of mint leaves, chopped
salt flakes and freshly ground black pepper
1 loaf sliced sandwich bread

**SERVES 8**

Cut the chicken into pieces about 1 cm thick. The delicious roasted skin can be included or not, depending on your preference.

Combine the almonds, celery, lemon zest and mayonnaise in a mixing bowl.

Add the chicken and herbs and stir through, then season to taste with salt and pepper.

Fill your sandwiches evenly with the chicken mixture, about 1 cm thick. Trim off the crusts, then cut each sandwich into three even fingers. An electric carving knife is perfect for this to avoid squashing the soft bread.

# MAC'N'CHEESE MUFFINS

One of the toughest jobs for parents is to pack our kids' lunchboxes with food that is unprocessed, healthy and delicious. This recipe is all of that, with plenty of energy to fuel your kids throughout the school day.

Everyone loves mac and cheese … so everyone loves mac and cheese muffins! You can get a little bit inventive and use your favourite type of cheese, but for my kids, the plainer the better. You can also use different sized muffin tins depending on how big you want them (just remember to adjust the cooking time). My son, Morgan, likes his muffins big!

These are also great to serve as part of a lunch platter when entertaining.

200 g (1⅓ cups) dried macaroni
50 g butter
50 g (⅓ cup) plain flour
500 ml (2 cups) milk
250 g (2 cups) grated cheddar
   and/or mozzarella
200 g baby spinach leaves
200 g ham, chopped
salt flakes and freshly ground
   black pepper
¼ bunch of chives, finely chopped

**MAKES 10**

Preheat the oven to 180°C (fan-forced). Grease a standard 12-hole muffin tin with butter and line with paper cases.

Cook the macaroni until al dente according to the packet instructions.

Meanwhile, melt the butter in a medium saucepan over medium–low heat, add the flour and cook, stirring, for 1 minute. Gradually add the milk, whisking constantly to remove any lumps. Stir gently and bring just to the boil, then reduce the heat to low and simmer for 2 minutes. Remove from the heat, add the grated cheese and stir until melted and smooth.

Wash the spinach leaves and wilt in a frying pan over medium heat for 30 seconds. Remove and roughly chop.

Drain the macaroni and return to the pan. Pour the cheese sauce over the pasta, add the spinach and ham and stir until everything is well coated. Season to taste and sprinkle with the chives.

Pour the mixture evenly into the prepared muffin tin and bake for 10 minutes. Serve warm or cool. Leftover muffins will keep in an airtight container in the fridge for up to 5 days. Gently warm through to serve.

These are also very good baked in a small cupcake tray to make 24 mini muffins, or go big and make six large Texas muffins.

# LITTLE FETA TARTS

Feta is one of my favourite cheeses in the world due to its texture and versatility. It goes well in salads but also with pastry; the feta seasons the pastry and gives it a great crumble.

You could also use this recipe to make one large tart and serve it with a nice green salad for a perfect brunch or lunch.

2 tablespoons dried breadcrumbs
150 g mixed coloured tomatoes, finely sliced into rounds
½ zucchini, finely sliced into rounds
1 yellow squash, finely sliced into rounds
1 tablespoon olive oil from the marinated feta (see below)
salt flakes and freshly ground black pepper
1 egg yolk, lightly beaten
a crisp green salad, to serve

**PASTRY**
225 g (1½ cups) plain flour, plus extra for dusting
100 g chilled unsalted butter, diced
50 g marinated feta
pinch of salt flakes
2 teaspoons finely chopped chives
1 large egg yolk, whisked with 80 ml (⅓ cup) chilled water

**FILLING**
100 g marinated feta, drained
300 g fresh ricotta, well drained
1 tablespoon chopped chives
finely grated zest of 1 lemon
1 egg
salt flakes and freshly ground black pepper

**MAKES ABOUT 10**

To make the pastry, place the flour, butter, feta, salt and chives in a food processor and pulse to the consistency of coarse breadcrumbs. Add two-thirds of the egg yolk mixture and process until the mixture starts to come together. Add more of the liquid if required.

Turn out the dough onto a lightly floured surface, bring it together with your hands and gently knead until smooth. Shape into a disc, wrap in plastic wrap and chill in the fridge for 15 minutes.

Preheat the oven to 220°C (fan-forced). Line two large baking trays with baking paper.

Meanwhile, to make the filling, combine all the ingredients – the mixture will be quite thick. Taste and adjust the seasoning if necessary.

Roll out the chilled dough on a lightly floured surface to a thickness of about 3 mm. Using a 10 cm cutter, cut out five discs. Transfer to one of the prepared baking trays, then sprinkle evenly with half the breadcrumbs, leaving a 1 cm border. Bring the dough scraps together, lightly knead, then rest for 5 minutes before re-rolling and cutting out another five or so discs. Transfer to the other prepared baking tray and sprinkle with the remaining breadcrumbs as above.

Spread or pipe the filling thickly over the breadcrumbs, then push the border pastry up and over the filling, leaving the centre exposed, pleating and pinching it in place. Using a palette knife, flatten the top of the filling until level.

Arrange the tomato, zucchini and squash slices over the filling, overlapping them so you can see the different colours. Drizzle with the oil from the marinated feta and season. Brush the pastry with egg yolk and bake for 20–25 minutes or until golden. Serve with a fresh salad.

# STEAK BANH MI

One of my favourite family holidays was spent in Vietnam. It is such a colourful place and a paradise for foodies; Vietnamese street food is among the best in the world.

Banh mi is simple to make at home. To make it easier to cut the beef into really thin slices, put it in the freezer and then slice from frozen. The beef 'shavings' will then cook really quickly and absorb the marinade, making for melt-in-your-mouth beef to combine with the crusty bread.

500 g porterhouse steak, placed in the freezer for 30 minutes
80 ml (⅓ cup) peanut, sunflower or vegetable oil
3 garlic cloves, crushed
salt flakes and freshly ground black pepper

**SESAME SAUCE**
2 tablespoons sesame oil
3 tablespoons hoisin sauce
2 tablespoons honey

**QUICK PICKLED VEGETABLES**
½ small red onion, finely sliced on a mandoline
½ small white onion, finely sliced on a mandoline
1 carrot, julienned
3 baby radishes, finely sliced on a mandoline
½ Lebanese cucumber, finely sliced lengthways on a mandoline
2 tablespoons rice wine vinegar
1 tablespoon white sugar
¼ bunch of mint, leaves picked and torn

**TO SERVE**
4 banh mi bread rolls
3 tablespoons chicken or duck pate
Japanese mayonnaise (kewpie)
sriracha chilli sauce (optional)

**SERVES 4**

Take the steak out of the freezer 10 minutes before slicing.

Preheat the barbecue to medium–high.

Using a chef's knife, finely shave the par-frozen meat. Place in a shallow bowl, add the oil and garlic and season generously with salt and pepper. Mix to coat well, then cover and marinate for a few minutes while you make the sauce.

For the sesame sauce, mix together all the ingredients in a medium bowl. Set aside.

Remove the beef slices from the marinade, shaking off any excess. Working in batches, quickly sear the meat on the hot barbecue for a few seconds each side. Remove and place in the sesame sauce. Set aside.

To make the pickled veg, combine all the vegetables in a large bowl. Add the vinegar and sugar and toss to coat, then stir through the mint.

When you're ready to serve, split the bread rolls down the middle and spread one side with pate and the other with mayonnaise and chilli sauce, if using.

Remove the beef from the sauce, allowing the excess to drip off, and add to the sandwich. Top with the pickled vegetables. Serve and eat immediately.

**TIP**

If you would like to give these a final flourish, julienne a couple of spring onions and soak them in iced water for 5 minutes until they start to curl. Drain and sprinkle over the banh mi before serving.

# SALADS
# & VEGETABLES

# MURCIAN SALAD CLASSICA

Just as the nicoise salad is an iconic dish from the south of France, the Murcian salad is a true staple of the southern Spanish city of Murcia, where I was born. It is on the menu in every tapas bar and every Murcian person knows how to make it.

This dish has everything you want from a salad: substance, flavour, texture and that homemade feel. The secret is crushing the tomatoes to create something between a sauce and a dressing. This is one of the only salads to showcase the humble white onion, as the acidity works in mysterious ways with the richness from the tomatoes.

My mama would make a massive batch of Murcian salad every week for the family to eat at different times of the day – in sandwiches, as a side to a main course or just on its own. We would devour it within days. Every mouthful of this salad – and even just looking at this photo – transports me to my homeland within seconds. It makes me so very proud to share something truly Murcian with Australian readers.

4 eggs
2 large oxheart tomatoes
400 g good-quality canned whole
   peeled tomatoes
½ white onion, very finely sliced
   on a mandoline
185 g good-quality canned tuna
   in olive oil (reserve the oil)
60 g (½ cup) pitted black olives
extra-virgin olive oil, for drizzling
salt flakes and freshly ground
   black pepper

**SERVES 4**

Boil the eggs for 6 minutes (for soft-boiled). Remove with a slotted spoon, reserving the water, and immediately place the eggs under cold running water to cool. Peel and set aside.

Cut a cross in the base of the tomatoes, then add to the pan of boiling water and blanch for 1 minute. Remove and cool in cold water, then peel and set aside.

To plate up, use your hands to crush the canned tomatoes and their juices into a salad bowl. Halve the eggs and arrange on top, then cut the tomatoes into quarters and add to the bowl. Top with the onion, flaked tuna and oil, and the olives. Dress with extra-virgin olive oil, season generously with salt and pepper and serve.

**TIP**

Always serve tomatoes at room temperature to appreciate their full flavour.

# STICKY SOY BARBECUED BROCCOLI
## WITH CORIANDER PESTO

*Gone are the days of basic boiled veggies; look at broccoli in a whole new light with this filling, flavoursome dish.*

2 heads of broccoli, quartered
100 ml kecap manis (Indonesian
  sweet soy sauce)
1 tablespoon sesame oil
2 tablespoons white sesame seeds
2 tablespoons grated palm sugar
1 teaspoon salt flakes
finely grated zest and juice
  of 1 lemon
lime cheeks, to serve
finely sliced radish and/or red chilli,
  to serve (optional)

### CORIANDER PESTO
1 bunch of coriander, leaves picked
  and roughly chopped
80 g (½ cup) toasted salted cashews
½ bunch of Vietnamese mint,
  leaves picked
80 ml (⅓ cup) extra-virgin olive oil
salt flakes and freshly ground black
  pepper (optional)

**SERVES 4**

To make the coriander pesto, place all the ingredients in a food processor and whiz to your preferred consistency. I like mine to still have a little texture. Taste and season if needed, then set aside.

Preheat a barbecue grill plate or a chargrill pan over medium heat.

Blanch the broccoli in a saucepan of boiling water for 30 seconds, then drain and tip straight into a large baking dish.

Whisk together the kecap manis, sesame oil, sesame seeds, palm sugar, salt, lemon zest and juice, then pour over the warm broccoli to coat well. Shake off and reserve the excess marinade, then grill for 2 minutes each side, basting with the reserved marinade. Grill the lime cheeks at the same time on a clean part of the grill.

Garnish with radish and/or chilli if you like, and serve with the grilled lime cheeks on the side.

# WATERMELON, FETA & MINT SALAD

I was once lucky enough to attend the Chinchilla Melon Festival in Queensland, where I took part in the watermelon olympics. No, this is not a typo … skiing with a watermelon on each foot and a pip-spitting competition were among the trials I had to endure. The best part for me, of course, was enjoying one of the most refreshing ingredients in the world.

It is amazing how versatile watermelon can be – in both sweet and savoury dishes. On a hot summer's day, watermelon with feta and mint, plus plenty of olive oil and freshly cracked pepper, is one of the best flavour combinations ever. This salad is the perfect way to wow friends or family when entertaining. Make sure you keep the geometrical shape of the cubes for a truly stunning presentation.

700 g watermelon, rind removed, cut into large cubes
200 g hard Greek feta, cut into cubes the same size as the watermelon
½ small red onion, finely sliced
2 tablespoons extra-virgin olive oil
1 tablespoon balsamic vinegar
½ bunch of mint, leaves picked
plenty of freshly ground black pepper

SERVES 4

This could not be easier. Put all the ingredients in a bowl, mix well and serve.

# CRUNCHY, CRISPY MUSHROOM BURGERS

Made with panko breadcrumbs for an extra crispy crumb, these baked-not-fried burgers are the healthier veggie version of your favourite KFC treat.

4 portobello mushrooms
250 ml (1 cup) buttermilk
75 g (½ cup) plain flour
30 g (½ cup) panko breadcrumbs
2 tablespoons chopped flat-leaf
    parsley leaves
½ teaspoon baking powder
1½ teaspoons Italian seasoning
1½ teaspoons garlic powder
1½ teaspoons smoked paprika
¼ teaspoon ground turmeric
¼ teaspoon cayenne pepper
    (optional)
1 teaspoon salt flakes
1½ teaspoons ground white pepper
1 teaspoon freshly ground
    black pepper
25 g butter, melted
soft bread rolls, cheese, lettuce and
    sliced tomato, to serve

## WASABI-SOY MAYO
3 tablespoons soy milk
1 tablespoon American mustard
1 tablespoon dijon mustard
1 teaspoon wasabi paste
1 tablespoon tomato sauce
250 ml (1 cup) vegetable oil
    or light olive oil

**SERVES 4**

Preheat the oven to 200°C (fan-forced). Place a large baking tray in the oven to heat up for about 10 minutes.

Place the mushrooms in a bowl and pour over the buttermilk to cover. Leave to sit for a couple of minutes.

Whisk together the flour, breadcrumbs, parsley, baking powder, dried herbs, ground spices, salt and white and black pepper in a medium bowl. Set aside.

Remove the mushrooms from the buttermilk, shaking off any excess, and dust in the seasoned flour mixture, coating them completely.

Remove the baking tray from the oven, then pour over the melted butter to coat the base. Arrange the mushrooms in the dish, well spaced and without touching the sides. Bake for 20 minutes, turning the mushrooms over halfway through.

Meanwhile, for the wasabi–soy mayo, put all the ingredients except the oil in a blender or food processor and blend until combined. With the motor running, gradually add the oil until thick and creamy.

Serve the baked mushrooms on soft bread rolls with cheese, lettuce, tomato and wasabi–soy mayo, or any of your favourite burger accompaniments. Store any leftover mayo in an airtight container in the fridge for up to 5 days.

# ZOODLES, CABBAGE & SESAME SALAD

A good-quality spiraliser is a game changer when it comes to raw veggies. This salad is one of my favourites to whip up after a day of eating lots of different rich foods. It is light, crunchy and fresh, and the chilli takes it to the next level. It is quick to make and goes well with any meat or grilled seafood.

The sesame dressing is easy to find in the Asian section of the supermarket. It is magic how the nuttiness of the sesame can turn this array of colourful veggies into a very pretty and healthy salad. Make sure you allow a little time for the dressing to soak into the cabbage for a better result.

¼ purple cabbage, finely sliced
¼ green cabbage, finely sliced
2 small carrots, spiralised
1 beetroot, spiralised
1 zucchini, spiralised
1 seedless cucumber, peeled and finely sliced into half moons
1 tablespoon sesame seeds
sliced chilli and furikake, to serve

**SESAME DRESSING**
splash of olive oil
100 ml roasted sesame kewpie mayo dressing
2 teaspoons sesame oil

**SERVES 4**

To make the dressing, combine all the ingredients in a small jug or bowl.

Place the purple and green cabbage in a bowl, add half the dressing and turn to coat well. Leave to marinate for 10 minutes.

To serve, spread the cabbage mixture over a plate and place the zoodles and cucumber on top, rolled up in little bunches. Drizzle with the reserved dressing and sprinkle with the sesame seeds, then finish with chilli and furikake to taste.

*Pictured on page 52.*

# QUINOA & SWEET POTATO SALAD

## IN A JAR

We all want to impress our colleagues with a packed lunch that shows just how gourmet and healthy we are.
Well, you will be the talk of the office when you bring out this jar salad, shake it till you make it and eat it,
perfectly dressed and combined, with no mess and no fuss. All you'll need is a fork.

This is the perfect way to use up dinner leftovers from the night before. You can get quite inventive with the formula,
just make sure you always start with the dressing in the base of the jar and don't tilt it or mix it until you're ready to eat.
This way, the salad will stay fresh and crisp until the last minute.

125 g canned corn kernels
100 g cooked quinoa
1 roasted sweet potato, diced
  (see Tip)
50 g goat's cheese, crumbled
handful of toasted walnuts
2 hard-boiled eggs, chopped
handful of baby rocket leaves

**DRESSING**
2 tablespoons balsamic vinegar
1 teaspoon freshly ground
  black pepper
1 tablespoon extra-virgin olive oil

SERVES 1

To make the dressing, whisk together all the ingredients in a mason jar (or similar).

Build your salad in the jar, starting with the dressing at the bottom. Layer in the corn, quinoa and sweet potato, followed by the cheese, walnuts, egg and finally the rocket. Close the jar and transport upright.

When you are ready to eat, gently shake the jar to coat the ingredients evenly in the dressing, then tip the salad onto a plate (or enjoy it with a fork straight from the jar).

*Pictured on page 53.*

**TIP**

To roast the sweet potato, dice and drizzle with extra-virgin olive oil, then roast in a 180°C (fan-forced) oven for about 30 minutes.

Zoodles, Cabbage & Sesame Salad, see page 50
Quinoa & Sweet Potato Salad in a Jar, see page 51
The Crunchiest Salad Ever with Buttermilk & Pangrattato, see page 54

# THE CRUNCHIEST SALAD EVER
## WITH BUTTERMILK DRESSING & PANGRATTATO

Simplicity and crunch are the two most important things when making a salad, and baby gem refreshed in iced water with celery leaves has both qualities. The buttermilk dressing has a very posh restaurant feel and the pangrattato (also known as poor man's parmesan) helps give everything a little more texture. I cook the eggs for six minutes so they stay nice and runny – they're a great way to make this dish a little more substantial.

The secret to this salad is to really drench the lettuce in looooots of dressing and then fully cover it with the pangrattato crumbs. I have served this salad at many of my restaurant events as it is pretty, holds well and never disappoints.

4 baby cos lettuce
handful of celery leaves
4 soft-boiled eggs, peeled
   and quartered
50 g (½ cup) shaved parmesan
anchovies, to garnish (optional)

### PANGRATTATO
2 tablespoons olive oil
60 g (¾ cup) fresh breadcrumbs
   (see Tip)
pinch of salt flakes
1–2 tablespoons finely chopped
   flat-leaf parsley, thyme and/
   or oregano leaves
finely grated lemon zest, to taste

### BUTTERMILK DRESSING
250 ml (1 cup) buttermilk
125 g (½ cup) mayonnaise
1 teaspoon lemon juice
½ teaspoon sweet paprika
1 teaspoon dijon mustard
½ teaspoon salt flakes
freshly ground black pepper
1 teaspoon chopped chives

**SERVES 6**

Cut the lettuce into quarters, then wash and refresh in iced water with the celery leaves for 2 minutes. Set aside to dry on paper towel.

For the pangrattato, heat the oil in a frying pan over medium heat. Add the breadcrumbs, season with salt and cook, stirring, until the crumbs have absorbed the oil. Stir in the herbs and cook for another 2 minutes or until the crumbs are golden. Season to taste with lemon zest, then tip into a bowl.

To make the dressing, mix together the buttermilk and mayonnaise in a bowl. Add the remaining ingredients, then taste and adjust the seasoning if needed.

To serve, place the cos and celery leaves on a plate, cut-side up. Top with the eggs, parmesan and anchovies, if using. Drench with the dressing and sprinkle the pangrattato generously over the top. Serve immediately.

*Pictured on page 52.*

 **TIP**

To make your own breadcrumbs, process torn pieces of crustless sourdough (or any stale bread) in a food processor until finely chopped. You can store any you don't use in the freezer for up to 3 months.

# MAMA FLORENTINA'S RUSSIAN SALAD
## WITH SPANISH OMELETTE

The Spanish version of this world-famous potato and mayonnaise salad is called Ensaladilla Rusa. One of my fondest food memories is of Mama and Papa making and decorating this together. When we were shooting this book, my mum sent me a picture of a Russian salad she'd made the day before and it looked exactly the same as the one here. I guess she taught me well! The two little figurines in this image are the huertanos from the Murcian festival El Bando de la Huerta. They symbolise my mum and dad.

The perfect way to serve Russian salad is with an old-school tortilla de patatas, another superstar recipe from Spain. Don't break up the potatoes during the frying process as you want to keep all those nice layers. A bit of confidence is required when it comes to flipping it – you just have to go for it. In Spain, some people love their tortilla de patatas undercooked in the middle, while others want this delicious morsel cooked all the way through – almost like a medium–rare versus well-done steak. You could make a trip to the Spanish deli before cooking this to get the most authentic ingredients. Try to get your hands on white anchovies (boquerones) and Cantabric anchovies (anchoas). For the full Spanish experience, please make your own mayo.

4 large potatoes, peeled, boiled
  and roughly chopped
2 carrots, peeled, chopped and
  boiled until tender
10 gherkins, finely diced
185 g canned tuna in olive oil
200 g fresh or frozen peas, blanched
10 white anchovies, 8 chopped,
  2 reserved for garnish
10 black anchovies, 8 chopped,
  2 reserved for garnish
285 g jarred piquillo peppers,
  drained and diced (reserve
  1 for garnish)
4 hard-boiled eggs, 2 quartered,
  2 grated to serve
200 g green olives, drained
salt flakes and freshly ground
  black pepper

**MAYONNAISE**
1 egg, straight from the fridge
250 ml (1 cup) extra-virgin olive oil
pinch of salt flakes
juice of 1 lemon

**SPANISH OMELETTE**
olive oil, for shallow-frying
2 onions, diced
4 small waxy potatoes, thickly sliced
12 eggs
pinch of salt flakes

**SERVES 8–10**

To make the mayonnaise, crack the egg into the beaker of a stick blender and add the remaining ingredients. Insert the stick blender, making sure it goes all the way to the bottom of the beaker, and blend until emulsified. Gradually move the blender up the beaker until your mayo is a nice creamy consistency.

Place the potato and carrot in a mixing bowl, then squash with a fork to make a mash. Add most of the mayonnaise (saving a little bit) and the gherkin, tuna, peas, chopped anchovy and diced piquillo peppers and mix well. Arrange on a plate and drizzle with the rest of the mayonnaise. Garnish with the quartered egg, reserved anchovies, reserved piquillo pepper, olives and grated egg and season with salt and pepper. Transfer to the fridge for a couple of hours to allow the flavours to meld.

For the Spanish omelette, heat a generous amount of oil in a large frying pan over medium–high heat, add the onion and potato and cook, without stirring so you don't break them up, until softened. Once the potatoes are cooked, drain off the excess oil.

Meanwhile, whisk the eggs in a mixing bowl. Add the potato mix, season with salt, then place the bowl in the fridge for 20–30 minutes before cooking.

Heat a generous splash of oil in large frying pan over high heat, add the egg mix and cook for 8 minutes until starting to crisp around the edge and almost set in the middle. Put a large plate over the pan and carefully flip it over. Reduce the heat to medium. Slide the omelette back into the pan and cook the other side for another 8 minutes or until set to your liking. Flip it back onto the plate and serve with the salad.

# MY FAMOUS PUMPKETTA

It has been a little bit of an obsession of mine to make a dish for vegetarians that replicates all the best parts of my delicious porchetta (see page 237), and this, ladies and gentleman, is one of my favourite inventions. I have trademarked this recipe as I feel so proud of it. If you are a vegetarian or a lover of veggies, this recipe will really hit the mark by showing you a different side to butternut pumpkin.

This is part recipe, part DIY project as you have to pop into a hardware store to get a PVC pipe and hammer. Yep, this is essential to keep the core of the pumpkin hollow without cutting it in half, giving the centre of the flesh direct contact with the heat to intensify its sweetness. Trust me, it makes it soooo different; it tastes like never before and every slice looks a million dollars. Just make sure the pumpkin isn't too green, otherwise it will be almost impossible to hollow it out.

Be energetic with the hammer and use the flesh from the centre in the stuffing so nothing is wasted. You can roast the seeds as well to make pesto, so it is truly nose-to-tail pumpkin usage. Roasting the pumpketta on a bed of rock salt is essential, as the salt helps to remove extra moisture from the skin.

1 small butternut pumpkin
    (about 1.2 kg)
1 egg
1 small red onion, finely chopped
1 garlic clove, crushed
small handful of flat-leaf parsley
    leaves, chopped, plus extra
    to serve
40 g (¼ cup) salted macadamia
    nuts, roughly chopped
50 g soft Persian feta, crumbled
185 g (1 cup) cooked brown
    jasmine rice (see Tip)
1 tablespoon olive oil, plus extra
    for drizzling
salt flakes and freshly ground
    black pepper
1 kg rock salt
hummus, pesto or baba ganoush,
    to serve

**SERVES 6**

Preheat the oven to 180°C (fan-forced).

Place the pumpkin upright on a chopping board (you may need to trim the base slightly so it sits straight). Using a piece of clean, hollow PVC pipe (about 25 cm long with a 4 cm diameter) and a hammer, hit the pipe through the centre of the pumpkin. Remove the pipe and the core of the pumpkin using the end of a wooden spoon. Grate the core and set aside.

Crack the egg into a medium bowl and whisk with a fork. Add the grated pumpkin, onion, garlic, parsley, macadamia, feta, rice and olive oil. Season with salt and pepper and mix to combine.

Spoon the mixture into the cavity of the pumpkin, using the end of a wooden spoon to pack it in tightly. Scoop any remaining filling onto a piece of greased foil and roll up to enclose.

Pour the rock salt into a small roasting tin. Rub the skin of the pumpkin with a little extra oil and salt flakes. Place the pumpkin and roll of filling on the rock salt and roast for 40 minutes, then turn over and roast for another 30–40 minutes or until just tender (the time will depend on the size of the pumpkin). Take care not to overcook it, otherwise it will be too soft to carve.

Remove the pumpkin from the oven and rest in the tin for 10 minutes. Transfer to a board and carve into slices. Serve with hummus, pesto or baba ganoush.

(TIP)

You can use microwave rice if you don't have leftover cooked rice.

# PATATAS BRAVAS

Every single venue in Spain serves patatas bravas as a tapa. The combination of simple fried potatoes and a spicy tomato sauce is a match made in heaven. I do mine a bit differently, with the sauce and aioli in the middle of the potato so you get some with every mouthful. Make sure you get the smallest chat potatoes you can – they should be bite-sized. Bravas means brave, and you have to be very brave to deal with this really spicy sauce!

80 ml (⅓ cup) extra-virgin olive oil, plus extra if needed
1 small onion, finely chopped
3 large ripe tomatoes, chopped
3 long red chillies, sliced
3 garlic cloves, sliced
1 teaspoon sherry vinegar
salt flakes
1 tablespoon smoked paprika
10 small chat potatoes, skin on, par-boiled
light olive oil, for shallow-frying
2 ½ tablespoons My Quick Aioli (see page 29)
finely chopped chives, to serve

**SERVES 4**

Heat 2 tablespoons of the olive oil in a small heavy-based saucepan over medium heat. Add the onion and cook for about 5 minutes until soft but not coloured. Add the tomato and cook for 5 minutes or until it begins to caramelise. Add the chilli and garlic and cook for another minute or so until fragrant.

Transfer the mixture to a blender (or use a stick blender), add the vinegar, salt, paprika and remaining oil and blend until smooth. Add more olive oil if needed to loosen the mixture.

Scoop out the centre of the cooked potatoes with a melon baller or measuring spoon, reserving the soft potato scoops.

Pour a generous amount of the light olive oil into a large frying pan, add the potatoes and reserved scoops and fry over high heat for 3–4 minutes or until golden brown.

Fill the potato shells with the bravas sauce, top with a teaspoon of aioli and garnish with chives. Serve hot with the crispy scoops on the side.

# WHOLE BAKED CAULIFLOWER
## WITH SWEET POTATO HUMMUS

I'm always looking for the perfect roast chicken substitute for vegetarians and this one is spot on. You can stuff a cauliflower like you would a chicken. The secret is to really take your time pushing the filling in with the back of a spoon – don't get frustrated, you want plenty of stuffing through the florets. This also makes the perfect side to roast beef for non-veggos!

1 head of cauliflower (about 1 kg)
boiling water, to cover
250 g frozen spinach, thawed
2 large eggs, lightly beaten
125 g canned corn kernels
2 tablespoons shredded
   basil leaves
2 tablespoons finely chopped
   chives, plus extra to serve
65 g (⅔ cup) grated parmesan
20 g (⅓ cup) panko breadcrumbs
125 ml (½ cup) thickened cream
salt flakes and freshly ground
   black pepper
80 g butter, melted
60 g mozzarella, grated

**SWEET POTATO HUMMUS**
1 large golden sweet potato
5 thyme sprigs, leaves picked
salt flakes and freshly ground
   black pepper
100 ml extra-virgin olive oil,
   plus extra to garnish
1 small garlic clove, roughly chopped
½ teaspoon ground cumin, plus
   extra to garnish
3 teaspoons tahini
180 g (1 cup) drained and rinsed
   canned chickpeas
juice of ½ lemon

**SERVES 4–6**

To make the hummus, preheat the oven to 250°C (fan-forced) or as high as your oven will go. Halve the sweet potato lengthways and score the cut side in a criss-cross pattern. Place, cut-side up, on a baking tray, then sprinkle with the thyme leaves, season well and drizzle with 1 tablespoon of the oil. Roast for 30 minutes or until soft. Remove and reduce the oven temperature to 200°C (fan-forced) for the cauliflower.

Scoop the sweet potato flesh out of the skin into a blender or food processor. Add the garlic, cumin, tahini, chickpeas, lemon juice and remaining oil and blend to your preferred consistency. Season to taste with salt and pepper and scoop into a bowl. Finish with an extra sprinkling of cumin and a drizzle of olive oil, then set aside.

While the sweet potato is roasting, trim the outside leaves and some of the inner stem from the cauliflower, taking care to leave it whole and without disturbing the florets. Place the cauliflower, stem-side up, in a large heatproof bowl or saucepan and pour over enough boiling water to cover. Set aside for 20 minutes to soften slightly.

Meanwhile, strain the spinach, pressing well to remove as much liquid as possible. Combine the spinach, egg, corn, basil, chives, half the parmesan and half the breadcrumbs, and mix in enough of the cream to make a loose mixture. Season well with salt and pepper.

Line a roasting tin with baking paper.

Drain the cauliflower well and place on a board, stem-side up. Spoon the spinach mixture a little at a time into the cauliflower, using your fingers or the back of a spoon to push it between the florets. Place the cauliflower, stem-side down, in the prepared tin.

Combine the melted butter with the remaining parmesan and breadcrumbs. Spread all over the cauliflower and season with salt and pepper.

Bake for 50–60 minutes or until tender. During the last 5 minutes, sprinkle evenly with the mozzarella and set the oven to grill to melt and brown the cheese.

Remove and stand for 10 minutes, then serve with the sweet potato hummus.

# TOMATO & BURRATA SALAD
## WITH PARMESAN WAFERS

Get creative with choosing your tomatoes for this salad. Any variety and combination will work, and all the amazing heirloom tomatoes we have available in Australia will really take your salad to the next level. The secret to this dish is having both the tomatoes and burrata at room temperature, so the fruit is full of flavour and the cheese is nice and oozy. Only break the burrata at the table – the theatre of it is the best part! Tear it open with your fingers in front of your guests.

200 ml balsamic vinegar
3 tablespoons brown sugar
50 g honey
500 g mixed heirloom tomatoes
salt flakes and freshly ground
    black pepper
extra-virgin olive oil, for drizzling
1–2 burrata balls, at room
    temperature
2 slices of sourdough bread
1 garlic clove, peeled and halved
½ bunch of basil, leaves picked

**PARMESAN WAFERS**
100 g (1 cup) grated parmesan

**SERVES 4**

For the wafers, line the base of a large frying pan with a piece of baking paper and heat over medium heat. Sprinkle one-quarter of the parmesan over the paper to form a 10 cm round (or thereabouts) and let it melt and bubble for about 2 minutes. Carefully lift the paper and cheese out of the pan and drape both over a rolling pin to cool in a curved shape. Repeat to make three more wafers, reusing the paper.

Place the vinegar, brown sugar and honey in a small saucepan and bring to a simmer over low heat. Cook, stirring occasionally, for 10 minutes or until reduced by about half. Set aside to cool.

Slice the tomatoes into different shapes and sizes and place on a large platter. Season generously with salt and pepper and drizzle with oil, then gently toss to combine. Place the burrata on top.

Toast the bread in a toaster, then rub with the cut side of the garlic while still warm. Drizzle with oil.

Scatter the basil over the tomato salad. Drizzle with oil and the balsamic reduction and serve with the parmesan wafers and toasted bread. Break open the burrata at the last minute.

# CREAMY PEA & HAM SOUP

This soup is great to make after Christmas using leftover ham, but you can cook it all year round using ham hocks available from the supermarket. The secret is to add the frozen peas right at the very end, then use a powerful blender to quickly combine as the less cooking and heating time the better to maintain that vibrant green colour.

250 g piece of fresh pancetta, diced
1 bunch of thyme, tied together with kitchen string
2 garlic cloves, finely chopped
1 bunch of spring onions, white part only, roughly chopped
½ bunch of celery, roughly chopped
2 leeks, white part only, well washed and roughly chopped
2 white onions, roughly chopped
2 ham hocks
3 litres chicken stock
10 thin slices of pancetta
500 g frozen peas
150 ml double cream
creme fraiche, to serve
40 g pork crackle, crushed, to serve
toasted sourdough, to serve

**SERVES 4–6**

Place the diced pancetta, thyme and garlic in a large saucepan over medium heat and cook, stirring, for 5 minutes or until golden brown. Add the spring onion, celery, leek and white onion and cook for 5 minutes until softened. Add the ham hocks and stock and bring to the boil, then reduce the heat and simmer for 2–3 hours.

Meanwhile, preheat the oven to 180°C (fan-forced).

To make crispy pancetta, arrange the finely sliced pancetta between two layers of baking paper, then place between two baking trays. Bake for 8 minutes, then remove from the oven, remove the top tray and paper and leave to cool and crisp up.

When the stock is ready, pull out the ham hocks and remove and shred all the meat. Set aside. Discard the thyme bundle, making sure none of the woody stems have escaped.

Add the peas and cream to the stock, then blitz with stick blender until smooth. To preserve the vibrant green colour, don't reheat the soup. Just stir in the reserved meat from the ham hocks and ladle into bowls.

Finish with a dollop of creme fraiche and garnish with crispy pancetta and crushed pork crackle. Serve with toasted sourdough.

# PASTA & RICE

# PAELLA A LA MAESTRE 2021

This is the recipe that defines me as a chef: the colour, the passion, the theatre, the intensity, the happiness. I've lost count of how many times I've made it in my many years behind the stove. The recipe evolves every year, which is why I include the year in the name – like your favourite vintage wine! Maestre is my mother Florentina's surname, and she is the one who first taught me how to make paella.

In Spain, there are more than 50 different ways to cook paella, depending on the region and the produce available. This way is my way, like the great Frank Sinatra said. After spending many years pursuing the perfect technique, I came up with this one, where I liquefy the sofrito to make a puree that defines the final flavour of the paella. It all came about at my restaurant, El Toro Loco, where I cooked paella to order. I had to come up with a way to achieve the perfect flavour balance in half the time and so, after much experimentation, the sofrito a la Maestre was born. The puree hits the pan with all the base flavours and becomes juicy and pulpy as the water from the tomato slowly evaporates. This is really the essential process when it comes to making a great-tasting paella. The dish itself is a blank canvas, and it is the addition of our amazing Australian seafood that makes it so delicious.

When all the stock has been absorbed, please cook the paella for an extra couple of minutes to achieve the soccarrada (the famous crust on the bottom of the pan). Serve the paella with loads of garlic aioli and enjoy the authentic Maestre experience. It's the very best of both Spain and Australia in one dish and it is my absolute favourite.

1 tablespoon olive oil
400 g (2 cups) Calasparra rice
2 litres fish or chicken stock, plus
   250 ml (1 cup water) if needed
salt flakes and freshly ground
   black pepper
10 black mussels, cleaned
   and debearded
4 king prawns, peeled and deveined
4 baby calamari hoods, cleaned
2 bugs, halved
10 pippies
4 scallops on the shell
100 g snapper fillet, skin and bones
   removed, cut into 2.5 cm cubes
2 lemons, halved
chopped flat-leaf parsley, to serve

## SOFRITO
150 ml extra-virgin olive oil
3 large, ripe oxheart tomatoes
5 jarred piquillo peppers
8 garlic cloves, peeled
½ bunch of thyme, leaves picked
½ bunch of flat-leaf parsley,
   leaves picked
1 bunch of chives, roughly chopped
1 teaspoon saffron threads
2 ½ tablespoons smoked paprika

**SERVES 4**

To make the sofrito, place all the ingredients in a food processor and process until smooth. If you don't have a food processor, roughly chop the tomatoes and piquillo peppers and finely chop the garlic, thyme, parsley and chives, then combine with the oil, saffron and paprika in a mixing bowl.

Heat the oil in a large paella pan over high heat. Add the rice and cook, stirring occasionally, for about 5 minutes or until it changes colour from white to transparent.

Stir in 12 large tablespoons (about 1 cup) of the sofrito (use any leftovers in a pasta sauce or freeze for another time) and cook for 3 minutes. Reduce the heat to medium, add the stock and season with salt and pepper, then cook, without stirring, for 5 minutes. Add all the seafood, spreading it out evenly for an attractive presentation, and cook for about 13 minutes or until the stock has been absorbed and the rice is almost tender. Add a splash of water if it gets a bit dry. Reduce the heat to low and cook, without stirring, for a further 3 minutes to form a nice 'soccarrada' or crust on the bottom. If your hob plate is not as big as the pan, move the pan around a little during cooking to ensure the crust forms evenly. Remove from the heat.

If there is still a little liquid, cover with a tea towel and leave for 2 minutes or so. Squeeze over some lemon juice and season to taste. Garnish with parsley and serve warm, not steaming hot.

# SWEET POTATO GNOCCHI
## WITH THYME & PINE NUTS

I learned how to make gnocchi from some of the best Italian chefs in the world, but for me, it's all about taking a classic dish and making it your own. Sweet potato is the most popular potato in Australia, and here it really turns this into something new. The secret is to add the flour gradually so the gnocchi remains really fluffy. Sweet potato can be either really wet or very dry so you need to use your fingers to judge how much or how little flour to add. When it comes time to cook the gnocchi, make sure all your ingredients are prepped and ready to go – just like a stir-fry. A little bit of excess cooking water will help loosen the sauce and stop the butter solids from burning, so always reserve some before draining.

2 sweet potatoes (about 450 g each)
salt flakes and freshly ground
   black pepper
300 g (2 cups) plain flour, plus
   75 g (½ cup) extra for mixing
   and dusting
olive oil, for pan-frying
40 g butter chopped
3 thyme sprigs, leaves picked
2 tablespoons pine nuts, toasted
lemon wedges, to serve

**SERVES 6-8**

**TIPS**

You can use gluten-free flour in the dough instead of plain flour if preferred. The butter can be replaced with coconut oil or a plant-based butter if dairy is an issue for you.

Preheat the oven to 200°C (fan-forced).

Using a fork, poke a few holes in the unpeeled sweet potatoes, then place directly on the oven rack and bake for 40 minutes or until tender. You will know they're ready when the skin is very wrinkly and a knife can be pressed easily into the centre. Alternatively, poke the sweet potatoes, wrap in damp paper towel and microwave in 2-minute bursts until very soft (allow 7–9 minutes, depending on your microwave).

Combine 2 teaspoons of salt and 225 g (1½ cups) of the flour on a work surface and make a well in the centre. Using tongs and a tea towel, open out the sweet potatoes and scrape the flesh into a bowl, discarding the skin. Mash with a potato ricer, mouli, potato mill, potato masher or fork (make sure there are no lumps if you're using a fork). Add the warm mash to the flour mixture, flour your hands and gradually work the sweet potato into the flour until well combined. You don't want the dough to be sticky so keep adding flour until you get a nice consistency. This might take a fair amount of flour if your potatoes were on the larger side.

Using a light touch, roll the dough into a ball and cut it into six to eight even pieces. Roll each piece into a long log about 1.5 cm thick. Cut into 2 cm lengths (roll them on a gnocchi board if you have one), then gently toss each piece in extra flour to ensure it's dry and not at all sticky. At this point, you can store the gnocchi in the fridge for up to 2 days, or freeze between layers of baking paper for up to 3 months.

Bring a large saucepan of salted water to the boil. Working in batches so you don't overcrowd the pan, add the gnocchi and cook for a couple of minutes until they float to the surface. Allow to boil for 30 seconds more, then remove with a slotted spoon and drain in a sieve set over a bowl. Reserve the cooking water.

Heat 2 tablespoons of oil in a large frying pan over medium heat, add the gnocchi and toss with the butter, thyme leaves and pine nuts until melted and well combined. Add a splash of the reserved cooking water to loosen things up if needed. Season to taste with salt and pepper and serve with lemon wedges.

# CALDERO MURCIANO

This is a very typical dish of Mar Menor, a small salt lake in my home city of Murcia. It is most closely associated with the two lakeside fishing villages of Cabo de Palos and Los Alcázares, where it is so special that it has its own day of honour. The recipe dates back to the nineteenth century, when the local fishermen used to prepare it on the beach (in the caldero or cauldron of the recipe title), using all the little fish that were not good enough to sell in the markets. I have fond childhood memories of my parents taking us to the amazing restaurants in these two small villages to enjoy this precious dish.

For my version I use Tasmanian crayfish, which is the jewel in the ocean's crown and has a truly sublime flavour. Presented in the shell like this, it's a dish to cook when you really want to impress someone for lunch – and I mean lunch, because this will send you straight to a siesta (especially when matched with a beautiful glass of bubbles). Try to get the very best quality Spanish rice and paprika you can. Make sure you slice the tail so everyone gets a piece of it, and enjoy it all with a big scoop of delicious ajo sauce.

1 large (600 g–1 kg) live lobster
250 ml (1 cup) extra-virgin olive oil
2 noras (see Tip)
400 g giant king prawns, unpeeled, heads removed and reserved
2 ripe tomatoes, peeled and chopped
2 litres chicken stock or water
2½ small heads of garlic, peeled and smashed separately
400 g (2 cups) Calasparra rice
salt flakes and freshly ground black pepper
200 g monkfish or flathead fillet, skin and bones removed, cut into 5 cm pieces

## AJO
1 small boiled potato, peeled
1 egg yolk
olive oil, for drizzling
salt flakes and freshly ground black pepper

SERVES 4–6

TIP

Noras are dried peppers, available from Spanish delicatessens. If you can't find them, use 2 tablespoons of smoked paprika instead.

Place the lobster in a plastic bag and leave it in the freezer for 1 hour to go to sleep.

Heat the oil in a large, heavy-based saucepan over high heat until smoking. Fry the noras for 1 minute, then remove and set aside. Fry the reserved prawn heads until pink, then remove and discard. Add the tomato and fry for 5 minutes, stirring occasionally, then pour in the chicken stock or water and bring to a simmer.

Separately smash the fried noras and one head of garlic using a mortar and pestle. Add them to the pot and cook for 5 minutes over high heat.

Blanch the lobster in the liquid for 7 minutes, then remove and cut in half. Remove the flesh from the shell (reserve the shell) and set aside in a bowl. Scoop out 250 ml (1 cup) of the stock and reserve.

Reduce the heat to low, add the rice to the remaining stock, season with salt and pepper and cook, stirring occasionally, for 20 minutes. Add the prawns in the last 4 minutes and the fish in the last 2 minutes.

Put the second smashed head of garlic in a food processor. Add the reserved stock and process until smooth. Pour over the lobster tails.

To make the 'ajo', which normally goes with this dish, smash the remaining half head of garlic and the boiled potato using a mortar and pestle. Add the egg yolk and beat well until smooth and creamy. While beating, add enough oil to achieve a consistency similar to mayonnaise. Season to taste.

To serve, fill the reserved lobster shells with rice and serve with lobster tails.

# THE PPP: PICI PASTA PESTO

If you want to get your family involved in making a dish from this book, this is the one! It doesn't matter how thick or thin the pici are rolled, the only thing that matters is the mantecare. This is the magical process of emulsifying the sauce with the residual pasta-cooking water. You need a really big mixing bowl and plenty of tossing and mixing to achieve this, and it is the one thing that will make your pasta perfect. Don't worry about anything else, just enjoy the family working together to create this classic pasta dish.

225 g (1½ cups) '00' flour or plain
   flour, plus extra if needed
2 pinches of salt flakes
1 teaspoon finely grated parmesan
3 tablespoons thickened cream
320 g mixed mini tomatoes, halved
1 tablespoon extra-virgin olive oil
small basil leaves and grated
   parmesan, to serve

**PESTO**
2 garlic cloves, peeled
2 pinches of salt flakes, or to taste
100 g (2 packed cups) freshly
   washed basil leaves, still wet,
   roughly chopped
2 tablespoons pine nuts, toasted
125 ml (½ cup) mild extra-virgin
   olive oil
3 tablespoons finely grated pecorino
3 tablespoons finely grated parmesan
freshly ground black pepper

**SERVES 4**

Store the leftover pesto in an airtight container, covered with a thin layer of oil. It will keep in the fridge for up to 1 week.

The amount of salt required for the pesto depends on the type of cheese you use. Some can be very salty so taste as you go. You can use 50 g (½ cup) of parmesan if you don't have any pecorino.

Place the flour, salt and parmesan in the bowl of a food processor, add 125 ml (½ cup) of warm water and process until the dough forms a ball. It should be smooth with the consistency of modelling clay, so add a little extra flour if needed. Wrap the dough and rest in the fridge so the gluten can relax, making it easier to roll out. Rest for at least 1 hour, though you can leave it for up to 24 hours.

To make the pesto, put the garlic and salt in a large mortar and use the pestle to pound to a paste. Add the basil and pine nuts in batches, and pound to break them up and form a paste. Gradually add the oil and mix until combined, then stir in the cheese. Taste and season with pepper and more salt if needed.

Pinch off a 2–3 cm piece of the rested dough and place between the palms of your hands. Roll into a log, then roll the log outwards with both palms, applying pressure evenly to form a noodle the same thickness as a fine pencil. Finish rolling on a clean surface (no extra flour) to the width of a fine green bean. Don't worry about being too precise – they are meant to be irregular. Place on a baking tray lined with baking paper and repeat with the remaining dough. (Alternatively, you can pat out the dough to a 3 mm thick rectangle and cut strips of dough, then roll, pressing lightly on each strip to roll it into a long worm shape about 3–4 mm thick.)

When you are ready to cook the pasta, bring a large, wide-based saucepan of salted water to the boil. Add the pasta and cook for 4–5 minutes until al dente.

Meanwhile, combine the cream, tomatoes and 3 tablespoons of the pesto in a large mixing bowl. Using tongs, transfer the cooked pici from the boiling water straight into the sauce, add the oil and toss to coat well.

Divide among bowls and serve topped with basil leaves and grated parmesan.

## VARIATION

For a chilli prawn pici, peel and butterfly 10 large king prawns, leaving the tails intact and reserving the heads and shells. Melt 60 g of butter in a saucepan over medium heat and cook the prawn heads and shells, crushing with a wooden spoon until you get a red-coloured butter. Strain and discard the heads and shells. Add a splash of olive oil to a large flameproof baking tray and cook the prawns over medium heat, without moving, for 2 minutes. Increase the heat to high, then toss through the pici, the red prawn butter and 2 finely sliced long red chillies until well combined and heated through. Sprinkle with half a bunch of basil leaves and serve.

# CHICKEN & CHORIZO PAELLA
## (THE AUSTRALIAN WAY)

There is something very special about this flavour combination that makes Aussie palates go loco. Narrow-minded chefs and food connoisseurs will tell you that you can't add chicken and chorizo to this dish and still call it paella, but in my many years in the food game I can tell you it has always been the most popular way to enjoy it here in Australia. And in fact, the first recorded paella recipe back in 1857 contained both chicken and chorizo (plus saffron, tomato, beans, pork, eel, peas and artichoke), and history doesn't lie!

The truth is, there are many different ways to make paella depending on the region: arroz negro uses squid ink, arroz con costra uses scrambled egg to create a crust on top, arroz caldoso is a little runnier with more sauce, and arroz al horno is baked in the oven. The chicken and chorizo version here, using this particular method for making the sofrito, originates in the Maestre house in Sydney, but it's just another spin on this beloved Spanish dish.

This is a much simpler paella recipe, making it a great midweek or entertaining dish in our land down under. In my opinion, this is a go-to meal to rival the classic bolognese, and will definitely become a family favourite. Make sure you buy the best quality chicken and chorizo you can (free range is the go). Try to use a proper paella pan and really push the cooking to the limit once all the stock is gone – this is how you achieve the famous crust on the bottom that will establish you as a real paella master.

250 g skinless chicken thigh fillets,
    cut into 2.5 cm cubes
2 chorizo sausages, finely sliced
    or diced
800 ml chicken stock
250 g (1¼ cups) Calasparra rice
50 g (⅓ cup) fresh or frozen peas
    (or snow peas or green beans)
salt flakes
½ bunch of chives, chopped
1 lemon, cut into wedges
My Quick Aioli (see page 29),
    to serve

### SOFRITO
4 oxheart or roma tomatoes,
    roughly chopped
4 large jarred piquillo peppers
4 garlic cloves, peeled
½ bunch of flat-leaf parsley,
    leaves picked
½ bunch of chives, roughly chopped
½ bunch of thyme, leaves picked
1¼ tablespoons extra-virgin olive oil
1 teaspoon saffron threads
1½ tablespoons smoked paprika

**SERVES 4**

To make the sofrito, place all the ingredients in a food processor and process until chunky. If you don't have a food processor, roughly grate the tomatoes, capsicums and garlic and roughly chop the parsley, chives and thyme, then combine with the oil, saffron and paprika in a mixing bowl.

Heat a 30 cm frying pan or paella pan over high heat, add the chicken and chorizo and cook for 5 minutes until golden brown. Add the sofrito and cook for 3–4 minutes until the tomato starts to break down and become juicy. Pour in the stock and bring to the boil. Stir in the rice and bring to a simmer, then continue to simmer for about 18 minutes.

When the rice is tender and most of the liquid has been absorbed (there should still be some liquid in the pan), add the peas or beans and cook, without stirring, for another 2 minutes to form a nice 'soccarrada' or crust on the bottom.

Season to taste with salt and garnish with chives. Squeeze over the lemon juice just before serving with aioli. Olé!

# MY FAVOURITE CHORIZO CARBONARA

Welcome to the most controversial Italian recipe in history. Purists, look away! I learned how to make this from Antonio Carluccio at the Good Food & Wine Show, but I have made it my own by using chorizo instead of the traditional guanciale. The oil from the chorizo gives it a special paprika colour and a Spanish twist.

It is important to toss the pasta with the eggs to create the creaminess from the egg yolk, without scrambling it. You need a really big bowl for this process, which is known as mantecare.

1 tablespoon extra-virgin olive oil
2 chorizo sausages, finely diced
2 garlic cloves, smashed and peeled
500 g bucatini, spaghetti, pappardelle or fettuccine
4 eggs
200 g (2 cups) grated Grana Padano or manchego (even better if you can find truffle manchego), plus extra to serve
salt flakes and freshly ground black pepper
green salad, to serve

SERVES 4

Heat the oil in a frying pan over medium heat, add the chorizo and cook until crisp and the red oil is released, taking care not to let it burn. Add one garlic clove, then remove the pan from the heat and let the residual heat gently cook the garlic.

Cook the pasta, along with the remaining garlic clove, for 1 minute less than recommended on the packet. It will finish cooking as you toss it with the sauce.

Meanwhile, lightly beat the eggs in a large bowl, mix through the cheese and season with salt and pepper. Add the chorizo and released oil and mix together well.

Using tongs, transfer the pasta straight from the pan into the bowl, allowing some of the pasta water to emulsify with the egg mixture. Toss very vigorously for 1 minute to coat all the pasta and ensure the egg stays smooth and creamy, and doesn't scramble.

Sprinkle with extra cheese and serve immediately with a side salad.

 **TIPS**

You can be experimental with the cheese. I use manchego, a Spanish sheep's milk cheese, for its nuttiness.

It is very important to use a good-quality chorizo. If you use low-quality chorizo, you will need to add smoked paprika to bring out the redness.

# VALENCIA PAELLA OF RABBIT,
## BEANS & ROSEMARY (THE SPANISH WAY)

The internationally renowned paella valenciana comes from the beautiful city of Valencia, home of the paella pan and countless incredible cooks, and which produces some of the best rice in the world. The amazing combination of ingredients includes rabbit (almost more commonly used than chicken in Spain, which may be why the Easter bunny never stops by my country), snails (the mussels of the land), rosemary, sweet paprika and garrafon (a delicious variety of butter bean). This is one of my favourites dishes in the world and really makes me proud to be Spanish.

At first glance, this picture looks like a really young and handsome version of me, but it's actually my little hermano (brother), Carlos. Our mother, Florentina, cooked plenty of paella valenciana for us growing up. It is really special to have Carlos appear in this book as he is my Spanish family in Australia and I love him dearly. At the end of the day, paella means one thing and one thing only to me and that's FAMILIA. I hope you can find the same meaning when you cook this very special dish for your family.

3 tablespoons extra-virgin olive oil
300 g chicken, skin on, bone in
(1 breast, cut into 3 portions,
2 drumettes, 1 thigh, halved)
300 g rabbit, skin on, bone in
(leg and ribs)
1 tablespoon smoked paprika
100 g snow peas, trimmed
100 g canned giant lima beans
(garrafon) or white beans
4 fresh artichoke hearts, cleaned
(see Tip)
1 large, ripe oxheart tomato, grated
2 litres chicken stock or water
salt flakes and freshly ground
black pepper
2 cups (400 g) Calasparra rice
2 rosemary sprigs
2 tablespoons sweet paprika
pinch of saffron threads, soaked
in a little water
15 snails (optional)

**SERVES 4**

Heat the oil in a 40 cm paella pan over high heat. Add the chicken and rabbit pieces and cook for 5–6 minutes or until golden brown all over. Add the smoked paprika and sauté quickly until fragrant, then add the the snow peas, lima beans and artichokes and cook for 1 minute. Add the tomato, reduce the heat to medium and cook, stirring, for 1 minute or until thickened slightly.

Pour in the stock or water and season with salt and pepper. Increase the heat to medium–high and cook, stirring occasionally, for 10 minutes or until the chicken and rabbit are cooked through.

Add the rice, rosemary, sweet paprika, saffron and snails, if using, and cook for 18 minutes. Reduce the heat to medium and cook, without stirring, for another 5 minutes to form a nice 'soccarrada' or crust on the bottom.

Remove from the heat and rest for 5 minutes before serving.

(TIPS)

To clean your artichokes, peel or cut away the dark outer leaves until you reach the soft, pale green leaves. Cut off the stem and the top third of the leaves, exposing the heart, then use a teaspoon to gently scrape out the hairy 'choke'.

Snails can be found at farmers' markets.

# PIES

# THE ONLY LAMB SHANK PIE
## YOU'LL EVER NEED

The one and only! This is something a bit different for all the pie lovers out there. The idea is to cook the lamb shanks until meltingly tender, so you can put one hand on the pastry and use the other to gently pull the bone out, leaving the delicious meat and sauce inside. Amazing!

4 lamb shanks, frenched, soaked
   in red wine overnight
plain flour, for dusting
salt flakes and freshly ground
   black pepper
2 tablespoons olive oil
350 g bacon, rind removed,
   roughly diced
3 carrots, diced
2 small onions, diced
6 portobello mushrooms, diced
2 leeks, white and pale green part
   only, well washed and diced
1 head of garlic, halved
   horizontally
5 rosemary sprigs
1.5 litres beef stock
2 sheets frozen puff pastry,
   chilled in the fridge
1 egg, lightly beaten
steamed greens or mushy peas,
   to serve

**SERVES 4**

Preheat the oven to 160°C (fan-forced).

Pat the lamb shanks dry, then dust in flour seasoned with salt and pepper, shaking off any excess.

Pour the oil into a flameproof casserole dish large enough to hold the four shanks in a single layer and heat over high heat. Brown the shanks well on all sides, then remove and set aside.

Add the bacon to the dish and cook for 3 minutes or until golden. Add the carrot, onion, mushroom, leek, garlic and rosemary and cook for 5–7 minutes, until soft and aromatic. Deglaze the dish with the stock, scraping up any bits caught on the base, and bring to the boil.

Return the lamb shanks to the dish, making sure they are completely covered by the vegetables and stock. Cover with foil or a lid, then transfer to the oven and bake for 2½ hours or until the meat is very tender and the sauce has thickened. Turn the shanks halfway through cooking.

Remove from the oven and increase the temperature to 180°C (fan-forced).

Place each lamb shank in an individual pie tin with a base measurement of 8–10 cm and spoon over the chopped vegetables and gravy. Squeeze the roasted garlic from the skins evenly into the tins.

Cut the pastry into four pie lids large enough to cover the tins and cut a hole in the middle for the lamb shank bone. Place the pastry over the filling, standing the shanks upright with the bones poking through the top. Brush the pastry with beaten egg and bake for 15–20 minutes until the pastry is puffed and golden. Serve with your choice of steamed greens or mushy peas.

# SPANISH MEAT PIE WITH WAGYU
## (WAGYU PASTEL DE CARNE)

In Spain, we use really good-quality beef in our pies. This is the pie I ate growing up – served on a paper napkin at the bar, cut in four, no plate, no sauce, just a cold beer! The combination of wagyu beef, chorizo and egg is sensational. This is definitely one to impress your friends and family with.

salt flakes and freshly ground
  black pepper
400 g wagyu scotch fillet or skirt
  steak, cut into 3 cm cubes
2 teaspoons plain flour
2 tablespoons extra-virgin olive oil
1 carrot, diced
1 onion, diced
1 leek, white and pale green part
  only, well washed and finely sliced
4 garlic cloves, chopped
5 black peppercorns, crushed
200 g chorizo sausages, finely diced
1 bunch of thyme, leaves picked
800 ml red wine
500 ml (2 cups) beef stock
4 sheets frozen puff pastry, thawed
1 egg, lightly beaten
4 hard-boiled eggs, quartered

**SERVES 4**

Season the beef, then dust in the flour, shaking off any excess.

Heat 1 tablespoon of oil in a medium saucepan over high heat. Add the beef in batches and cook until browned all over. Remove and set aside.

Reduce the heat to medium and add the remaining oil. Add the carrot, onion, leek, garlic, peppercorns, chorizo and thyme and cook, stirring occasionally, for 10 minutes or until the vegetables are soft.

Return the beef to the pan, pour in the wine and cook until reduced by half, scraping up any bits caught on the base. Add the stock and bring to the boil, then reduce the heat and simmer for about 1½ hours until the meat is tender and a thick gravy has formed. Set aside to cool completely.

Preheat the oven to 200°C (fan-forced). Grease four pie tins with a base measurement of 8–10 cm.

Cut out eight 13 cm circles from the pastry. Use four circles to line the base and side of the pie tins. Trim the edges, then line with baking paper and fill with uncooked rice or baking beans. Blind-bake for 10 minutes, then remove the paper and weights and brush the pastry with beaten egg. Bake for another 8 minutes, then set aside to cool.

Divide the cooled filling and hard-boiled egg evenly among the pastry cases. Top with the remaining pastry rounds, trim the edges and press with a fork to seal. Brush with the remaining beaten egg and bake for 15 minutes or until the pastry is puffed and golden and the filling is hot.

(TIPS)

The beef filling can be made up to 2 days ahead and stored in an airtight container in the fridge.

Use fresh puff pastry if you can find it.

*Fun Guy Chicken Pie, see page 98*
*Creamiest Snapper Pie, see page 99*

# FUN GUY CHICKEN PIE

Australians love the combination of chicken and mushroom. This simple dish is a true one-pot wonder. It's creamy, delicious and perfect for a midweek dinner. This is a bulletproof recipe that I guarantee will become a family favourite.

1 tablespoon olive oil
40 g butter
1 onion, grated
1 carrot, grated
1 tomato, finely diced
600 g chicken thigh fillets,
    cut into 2.5 cm cubes
1 tablespoon plain flour
100 g swiss brown mushrooms,
    sliced
1 teaspoon dijon mustard
2 tablespoons creme fraiche
    (or thickened cream)
350 ml chicken stock
a few thyme and rosemary sprigs
½ teaspoon ground or freshly
    grated nutmeg
salt flakes and freshly ground
    black pepper
50 g grated cheddar
1 sheet frozen puff pastry, thawed
1 egg, lightly beaten
green salad, to serve

**SERVES 4**

Preheat the oven to 170°C (fan-forced).

Heat the oil and half the butter in a flameproof pie dish or round baking dish over medium heat, add the onion, carrot and tomato and cook for a few minutes until softened.

Add the chicken, flour and remaining butter and cook, stirring, until nicely browned all over. Add the mushroom, mustard, creme fraiche and stock and stir well to combine. Add the thyme, rosemary and nutmeg, season with salt and pepper and simmer for 4 minutes or until the sauce has thickened slightly.

Take the dish off the heat and sprinkle over the cheese. Remove and cool in the fridge for 10 minutes, then cover the filling with the puff pastry. Trim off the excess and crimp around the edge to seal. Brush with the beaten egg and bake for 15 minutes, or until puffed and golden. Serve with a fresh salad.

*Pictured on page 97.*

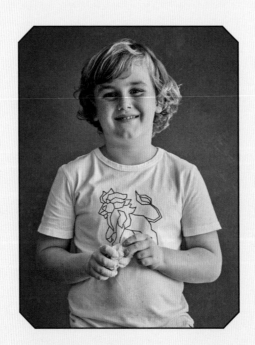

# CREAMIEST SNAPPER PIE

People either love or hate fish pie, but I think this recipe will get a few more lovers on side. There's something so charming about the silkiness of the white sauce with the tender fish, and the breadcrumbs sprinkled over the mash add texture while giving a rustic look to the potato peaks. You need super fresh fish for this recipe, but feel free to swap the snapper for salmon, kingfish, cod or flathead, and you can leave out the prawns if they don't jingle your bells.

2 teaspoons olive oil
2 large onions, sliced
1 small leek, white part only, well washed and diced
salt flakes and freshly ground black pepper
40 g butter
1 ½ tablespoons plain flour
300 ml milk
finely grated zest of ½ lemon
2 tablespoons dijon mustard
2 thyme sprigs, leaves picked
small handful of tarragon leaves, finely chopped
600 g snapper fillet, skin and bones removed, cut into 3 cm chunks
300 g fresh prawn meat, roughly chopped
2 tablespoons panko breadcrumbs

**MASHED POTATO**

700 g desiree potatoes, peeled and cut into 4 cm cubes
2 teaspoons salt flakes
40 g butter
2 tablespoons milk

**SERVES 4**

Heat the oil in a large saucepan over medium heat, add the onion, leek and a pinch of salt and cook for 10–15 minutes until very soft and sweet but not browned. Cover and keep warm until needed.

Melt the butter in a small saucepan over low heat and sprinkle in the flour, stirring vigorously. Cook for a couple of minutes until the flour smells toasty, then gradually add the milk, whisking constantly until smooth and combined. Keep stirring until the sauce is the consistency of thickened cream. Stir in the lemon zest, mustard and herbs.

Pour the sauce over the onion mixture, taste for seasoning and adjust if necessary. Cover and chill in the fridge until the mash is ready.

Meanwhile, for the mashed potato, place the potato in a large saucepan, cover with cold water and add the salt. Bring to the boil over high heat, then reduce the heat to medium and cook for 20–25 minutes until completely tender. Drain, then mash with a masher or ricer. Add the butter and milk and whisk until smooth. Cover and chill in the fridge.

When you're ready to cook the pie, preheat the oven to 175°C (fan-forced).

Stir the fish and prawn meat into the cooled sauce, then scoop into a 1.5 litre pie dish. Dollop the mashed potato on top and smooth with a spatula (or use a piping bag fitted with a star nozzle). Sprinkle the breadcrumbs evenly over the potato and bake for 35 minutes or until the potato is golden, the seafood is cooked and the sauce is hot.

*Pictured on page 96.*

# CHORIZO & BEEF EMPANADILLAS

In Spain, we have different stages of eating throughout the day. Between breakfast and lunch we have almuerzo, a kind of morning tea or brunch. I have the best memories of eating these empanadillas for almuerzo growing up. We'd cut them open and put heaps of mayo inside so they were really juicy. These are really easy to make and perfect for snacks or lunchboxes.

6 sheets frozen puff pastry, thawed
olive oil, for pan-frying
2 small onions, finely diced
3 garlic cloves, finely chopped
½ small red chilli, deseeded and
   finely chopped
pinch of ground cumin
pinch of ground cinnamon
½ teaspoon smoked paprika
250 g beef mince
250 g chorizo sausages,
   finely chopped
salt flakes and freshly ground
   black pepper
80 g (⅓ cup) pitted green olives,
   chopped
1 teaspoon dried oregano
pinch of sugar
4 hard-boiled eggs, finely chopped
2 large eggs, lightly beaten

## KALE AND PARSLEY SAUCE
1 bunch of flat-leaf parsley,
   leaves picked
handful of kale leaves
3 garlic cloves, peeled
1 teaspoon dried oregano
1 teaspoon dried chilli flakes,
   or to taste
1 tablespoon red wine vinegar
1 tablespoon lemon juice
100 ml extra-virgin olive oil
salt flakes and freshly ground
   black pepper

**MAKES 24**

Lay the pastry sheets out on a clean work surface. Using an 11 cm cutter or small plate, cut out 24 rounds. Place on large baking trays, well spaced out, and cover with plastic wrap or a clean tea towel. Chill in the fridge while you prepare the filling.

Heat a little oil in a medium saucepan over medium heat, add the onion, garlic and chilli and cook for about 5 minutes until soft but not coloured. Add the cumin, cinnamon and paprika and stir until aromatic.

Add the beef and chorizo, season with salt and pepper and cook for about 5 minutes until lightly browned, breaking up any large lumps with the back of a wooden spoon. Mix in the olives, oregano, sugar and hard-boiled egg, then taste and adjust the seasoning if necessary. Set aside to cool completely.

Line two large baking trays with baking paper.

Spoon about 1 tablespoon of the cooled filling onto each pastry round, leaving a 1 cm border around the edge. Brush half the border with beaten egg, then fold the pastry over and press the edges together to seal and create a half-moon shape, crimping and removing any air pockets as you go. Transfer the empanadillas to the prepared trays and place in the fridge for 20 minutes to firm up.

Preheat the oven to 190°C (fan-forced).

Using a skewer, make a steam hole in the top of each empanadilla, then brush with beaten egg. Bake for 20–25 minutes until the pastry is puffed and golden.

Meanwhile, to make the sauce, place the parsley, kale and garlic in a small food processor and roughly chop. Add the oregano, chilli, vinegar, lemon juice and oil and blitz briefly to combine. Season to taste with salt and pepper.

Remove the empanadillas from the oven and cool on a wire rack. Serve warm or at room temperature with the kale and parsley sauce.

# FAMILY HEIRLOOM SPANISH CHICKEN PIE
## (PASTEL DE CIERVA)

Pastel de Cierva is a popular Spanish pie that combines sweet and salty in a unique way. It is originally from the Mar Menor region in Murcia, my home town, and has a strong connection to my family. One of my ancestors, Jose Maestre (a famous doctor and politician), wanted to impress one of his very influential guests, Juan de la Cierva, inventor of the helicopter. He asked the local pastry chef to make this recipe and name it in honour of the famous inventor.

The combination of sugar and suet in the pastry is so unique. It makes the pastry very short and crumbly, which works brilliantly with the chicken filling. You can get suet from any butcher.

1 x 1 kg chicken
250 g pork fat or lard,
   at room temperature
250 g caster sugar
finely grated zest of 1 lemon
2 eggs
450 g (3 cups) plain flour
2 hard-boiled eggs, chopped
1 egg, lightly beaten

**SERVES 4-6**

Place the chicken in a large saucepan or stockpot. Cover with cold salted water and bring to the boil, then reduce the heat and simmer gently for about 1 hour or until cooked through. Remove the pan from the heat and leave the chicken to cool in the liquid for 30 minutes. Remove the chicken and reserve 250 ml (1 cup) of the liquid. Refrigerate until cold, then remove the skin and bones and shred the meat. Combine with enough of the reserved poaching liquid to give a slightly wet consistency.

Preheat the oven to 200°C (fan-forced).

Place the pork fat or lard and sugar in the large bowl of a stand mixer fitted with the paddle attachment. Beat for 2 minutes or until light and fluffy, then beat in the lemon zest. Add the eggs one at a time, beating between additions. Gradually add the flour and beat to just combine and form a dry-ish dough. Allow the pastry to rest for 15 minutes.

Turn out the dough onto a clean surface and divide in half. Roll out one half between two sheets of baking paper until 1 cm thick and large enough to line the base and side of a 23 cm loose-based flan tin. Line with baking paper and fill with uncooked rice or baking beans, then blind-bake for 20 minutes. Remove the paper and weights, then fill with the shredded chicken and boiled egg.

Roll out the remaining piece of dough between two sheets of baking paper until large enough to cover the pie. Trim the edges and press with a fork to seal. Brush the top with beaten egg and bake for 40 minutes or until the pastry is golden and crisp. This is best eaten on the day of baking, so get stuck in!

# CHORIZO SAUSAGE ROLLS
## (SALADITOS)

There's nothing worse than a dry sausage roll. My Spanish take on the classic uses chorizo sausage, which has plenty of natural oils to make the rolls juicy and flavoursome every time. This is my kids' favourite lunchbox treat (and their papa's, too).

5 garlic cloves
2 pork and fennel sausages
5 chorizo sausages, casing
  removed, chopped
3 tablespoons pistachio kernels,
  toasted and finely chopped
200 g manchego cheese, grated
1 bunch of chives, finely sliced
1 teaspoon freshly ground
  black pepper
4 sheets frozen puff pastry, thawed
2 eggs, lightly beaten
tomato sauce, to serve

**MAKES 24**

Preheat the oven to 180°C (fan-forced). Wrap the garlic cloves in foil and roast for 30–40 minutes until very soft. Squeeze out of their skins and mash.

Remove the casings from the sausages and place the sausage meat in a large bowl. Add the chorizo, mashed garlic, pistachios, manchego, chives and pepper and mix together well with your hands.

Cut each pastry sheet in half. Roll 125 g of the sausage mixture into a log shape the same length as the pastry. Lay the mince along one long edge of pastry and lightly brush the other long edge with egg. Roll the pastry to enclose the filling and press gently to seal. Repeat with the remaining pastry and filling. Place in the fridge for at least 1 hour to firm up. (Keep the rest of the egg wash for later.)

Preheat the oven to 200°C (fan-forced). Line a large baking tray with baking paper.

Cut each roll into three even pieces, brush with the reserved egg and grind over some fresh pepper.

Place, seam-side down, on the prepared tray and bake for 25–30 minutes until golden and cooked through. Serve with tomato sauce.

# FISH & SEAFOOD

# BARBECUED JAMON-WRAPPED KING PRAWNS

Australian king prawns are the best in the world and they pair perfectly with jamon. The salty ham seasons the prawns, and once it crisps up on the barbecue the texture contrast is amazing. This is surf and turf on a skewer!

3 tablespoons chopped flat-leaf parsley leaves

3 tablespoons extra-virgin olive oil

1 long red chilli, deseeded and finely chopped

2 garlic cloves, finely chopped

12 raw king prawns, peeled and deveined, heads and tails intact

12 slices of jamon

**ROMESCO COULIS**

10 blanched almonds, toasted

3 jarred piquillo peppers

½ cup (15 g) coriander leaves

1 garlic clove, chopped

1 long red chilli, chopped

1 tablespoon extra-virgin olive oil

1 tablespoon lemon juice

salt flakes and freshly ground black pepper

**SERVES 4**

Combine the parsley, oil, chilli and garlic in a shallow bowl.

Wrap the body of each prawn in a slice of jamon. Place the prawns in the parsley marinade and turn to coat. Cover and marinate in the fridge for 2 hours.

If you are using wooden skewers to grill the prawns later, soak them in water for a couple of hours so they don't burn or fall apart during cooking.

To make the romesco coulis, place all the ingredients in a blender or food processor and blend until smooth. Taste and adjust the seasoning if necessary. Depending on when you make this, store it in the fridge until needed. It will keep in an airtight container for up to 5 days. Just be aware that it needs to be out of the fridge for at least an hour before eating so it is served at room temperature. If you try to use it straight from the fridge it will be too firm and the oil will be set on top.

Preheat a barbecue grill plate or chargrill pan over medium heat. Thread each prawn onto a small skewer and cook for 2–3 minutes on each side until cooked through with an orange colour around the heads and tails. Serve with the romesco coulis.

# OYSTERS THREE WAYS

Australia is home to the best oysters I've ever tasted as a chef, which is lucky for me as oysters are my favourite way to start a meal. Here are three very different options guaranteed to please and impress your guests. In my family, every big occasion or get-together starts with these bloody mary shots.

**MAKES 18**

## BLOODY MARY OYSTERS

100 ml tomato juice
9 drops of Tabasco sauce, or to taste
3 dashes of Worcestershire sauce
juice of ½ lime
6 shots of vodka (optional)
freshly ground black pepper
6 oysters, removed from the shell
young celery sticks, to serve

Before you start, make sure all the ingredients are chilled.

Combine the tomato juice, Tabasco, Worcestershire sauce, lime juice and vodka, if using, in a small jug. Season well with pepper.

Put each oyster in a shot glass and pour over the bloody mary mix. Serve garnished with celery sticks.

## TEMPURA OYSTERS
### WITH WASABI MAYONNAISE

vegetable oil, for deep-frying
180 ml chilled water
125 g store-bought tempura batter mix
6 oysters, removed from the shell
125 g (½ cup) Japanese mayonnaise (kewpie)
2 teaspoons wasabi paste
salt flakes
baby coriander leaves, to serve

Pour the oil for deep-frying into a medium saucepan over medium–high heat and heat to 180°C.

Pour the chilled water into a medium bowl and add the tempura batter mix. Whisk to combine, without over-mixing.

Dip the oysters in the batter, gently add to the oil and deep-fry for 2 minutes or until crisp and golden. Remove and drain on paper towel.

Meanwhile, mix together the mayonnaise and wasabi paste in a small bowl.

Put a dollop of wasabi mayo in the base of six flat spoons, top with a tempura oyster, sprinkle with salt and garnish with coriander leaves.

## FRESH OYSTERS
### WITH PICKLED GINGER

6 oysters, on the shell
rock salt, for serving
125 g (½ cup) sesame seaweed salad (from a sushi restaurant)
3 tablespoons finely shredded pickled ginger
1 tablespoon soy sauce

Arrange the oysters on a plate of rock salt (so they don't wobble) and top with seaweed salad, pickled ginger and a dash of soy.

# SALT & PEPPER CALAMARI ROLLS

In Australia, we think of salt and pepper calamari as a standard fish and chip shop offering, but in Spain, it's one of the most common sandwich fillings. It might seem strange, but once you try it you'll never go back! Super soft white bread rolls and plenty of aioli are essential. Best. Sandwich. Ever.

3 tablespoons mixed peppercorns (pink, green, black, Sichuan)
1 teaspoon salt flakes
60 g (⅓ cup) rice flour, plus extra if needed
50 g (⅓ cup) plain flour, plus extra if needed
8 small calamari, cleaned and finely sliced
light olive oil, for shallow-frying
4 very, very soft white rolls
My Quick Aioli (see page 29), to serve
1 lemon, cut into wedges

**SERVES 4**

Using a mortar and pestle, pound the peppercorns and salt until well crushed, but with some texture remaining. Combine the peppercorns and both flours in a large zip-lock bag. Add half the calamari and shake until evenly coated (if the mix is too dry, add a little more flour). Remove to a plate. Repeat with the remaining calamari.

Heat 1 cm of oil in a large frying pan over high heat. Working in batches, add a single layer of calamari and cook for 1–1½ minutes, turning halfway through, until golden. Remove and drain on paper towel. Repeat with the remaining calamari.

Cut the bread rolls in half and pile in the calamari. Add aioli and lemon juice to taste and demolish immediately.

# CRISPY SKINNED SNAPPER
## WITH SAUCE GRIBICHE

*Most people don't eat fish skin because they don't achieve the right level of crispiness and texture. If you cook it properly you'll never leave it behind – it's like pork crackling, the best bit! The secret is to dry the skin thoroughly with paper towel and score it with a very sharp knife. Always place a piece of baking paper between the fish and the surface of the pan to allow the skin to slowly crisp without burning.*

2 x 250 g baby snapper fillets (whole sides from a 600 g–1 kg fish), skin on, bones removed (see Tip)
salt flakes and freshly ground black pepper
2 teaspoons extra-virgin olive oil
25 g butter

### SAUCE GRIBICHE
4 large eggs
1 tablespoon baby capers, roughly chopped
6 cornichons, finely chopped
1 garlic clove, finely chopped
1 small golden shallot, finely chopped
1 tablespoon finely chopped chives
2 tarragon sprigs, leaves picked and chopped
2 tablespoons roughly chopped flat-leaf parsley leaves
2 teaspoons dijon mustard
splash of extra-virgin olive oil
salt flakes and freshly ground black pepper
splash of sherry vinegar

### SPRING VEGETABLES
100 g baby beans, trimmed
75 g podded fresh peas
100 g snow peas, trimmed
1 small golden shallot, shaved into rounds
splash of extra-virgin olive oil
splash of sherry vinegar
salt flakes and freshly ground black pepper

**SERVES 2**

To make the sauce gribiche, cook the eggs in boiling water for 6 minutes, then cool immediately in iced water to stop the cooking process. Peel the eggs and mash. Add the chopped capers and cornichons, garlic, shallot, fresh herbs, mustard and oil and whisk everything together. Season with salt and pepper and add enough vinegar to balance the flavours. Set aside.

For the spring vegetables, blanch the beans in a large saucepan of boiling water for 2 minutes or until just tender, adding the peas and snow peas for the last minute of cooking. Refresh in iced water, then drain and place in a bowl. Add the shallot, oil and vinegar, season with salt and pepper and toss to combine.

Pat the snapper fillets dry with paper towel, then score the skin with a sharp knife. Season with salt and pepper.

Cut out a piece of baking paper to fit the base of a medium frying pan. Add the oil to the pan and heat over medium heat. Place the paper on the base, then immediately put the snapper fillets on top, skin-side down.

Press the fish into the pan with an egg flip to ensure maximum crispness, and prevent it from curling up. Keep the heat at medium – if it becomes too hot the skin will burn before the fish is cooked through. Cook until the sides of the fillets change from white to golden, basting the fish with the pan juices. After 2–3 minutes, add the butter and flip the fillets over. Cook for just 30 seconds, basting with the butter, then remove from the heat.

Divide the vegetables between two plates and top with the snapper and the sauce, then serve.

**TIP**

This recipe works best with fresh fillets of snapper; the fish may stick if thawed from frozen.

# POPCORN FISH TACOS
## WITH CORN SALSA

Australians are in love with Mexican food and fish tacos are the dish of choice at Mexican restaurants around the country. My version uses popcorn crumbs to give the fish texture without overpowering its flavour. Baja is one of my favourite sauces to serve with tacos. Everyone knows guacamole and salsa, but trust me, baja will take your tacos to the next level and make them very authentic. It is essential to warm the soft tortillas over an open flame to allow them to puff up again. Please don't warm them in the microwave!

1 ripe avocado
¼ teaspoon lime juice
splash of extra-virgin olive oil
1 teaspoon sour cream
salt flakes and freshly ground
　black pepper
6 soft tortillas
6 hard taco shells

### CORN SALSA
3 tablespoons extra-virgin olive oil
2 corn cobs, silks removed, kernels
　cut off
2 ripe field tomatoes, cores
　removed, cut into dice the size
　of corn kernels
½ bunch of coriander, leaves
　picked and roughly chopped
½ red onion, cut into dice the size
　of corn kernels
juice of 1 lime
1 fresh (or pickled) jalapeno,
　deseeded and diced
salt flakes and freshly ground
　black pepper

### BAJA SAUCE
10 pickled green peppercorns
1 fresh (or pickled) jalapeno chilli,
　deseeded and roughly chopped
¼ bunch of coriander, leaves
　picked and roughly chopped
juice of 1 lime
3 tablespoons sour cream
1 tablespoon extra-virgin olive oil
salt flakes

### POPCORN FISH
150 g (1 cup) plain flour
3 eggs

50 g lightly salted popcorn,
　blended to a coarse crumb
　in a food processor
400 g firm flathead fillets, skin and
　bones removed, cut into 6 cm x
　3 cm pieces
sunflower oil, for shallow-frying
salt flakes and freshly ground
　black pepper

### MAKES 6

To make the corn salsa, heat 1 tablespoon of the oil in a medium saucepan over high heat. Add the corn and cook, stirring occasionally, for 2 minutes or until coloured and just tender. Tip into a bowl, add the remaining ingredients and mix well. Taste and adjust the seasoning if needed, then set aside.

For the baja sauce, using a mortar and pestle, pound together the peppercorns, chilli, coriander and lime juice to form a rough paste. Stir in the sour cream and oil and season to taste with salt. Set aside.

Cut the avocado in half, remove the seed but don't throw it away. Divide the lime juice, oil and sour cream between the two halves and mash with the flesh to form a rough guacamole. Season to taste with salt and pepper. To preserve the green colour, return the seed to the centre of the avocado

and gently press the two halves together until you're ready to serve.

To make the popcorn fish, tip the flour onto a plate, beat the eggs in a bowl, and spread the popcorn crumb over a second plate. Working with one piece of fish at a time, dust in the flour, shaking off the excess, then dip in the egg, allowing the excess to drip off. Finally, toss in the popcorn crumb, making sure it is evenly coated. Set aside on a clean plate.

Pour the oil into a large, deep frying pan to a depth of 4 cm and heat over medium–high heat to 200°C. Test the oil with the handle of a wooden spoon to see if bubbles appear. Add the fish in batches and fry for 2 minutes on each side or until golden and cooked through. Drain on paper towel and season with salt and pepper.

To assemble, spread a spoonful of guacamole in the centre of a soft tortilla. Place a hard taco shell on top and gently press the two together, using the guacamole as glue. Set aside and repeat with remaining taco shells and tortillas.

Spoon some salsa into the base of each hard taco, top with the popcorn fish and drizzle over the baja sauce. Eat immediately.

*Seared Scallops, see page 120*
*Bazza's Symi School Prawns with Greek Salad, see page 121*

# SEARED SCALLOPS

I'm a seafood chef by trade and scallops are definitely the hardest shellfish to cook perfectly. My method is to add them all to a smoking hot pan at exactly the same time, so that they sear rather than stew. You want to achieve the beautifully caramelised ring known in restaurant kitchens as 'the crown'. Scallops are the jewels in the crown, so they need to be treated as such!

1 bunch of chives, finely chopped
10 basil leaves, finely chopped
splash of extra-virgin olive oil, plus
    extra for pan-frying and to serve
finely grated zest and juice
    of 1 lemon
25 scallops on the shell
250 g rock salt

**SERVES 4–6**

Combine the chives, basil, oil, lemon zest and lemon juice in a bowl.

Remove the scallops from the shells and divide among three pieces of baking paper, placing them close together. Wash the shells for presentation and arrange on a large platter.

Heat a splash of oil in a large frying pan over very high heat until smoky. Once it's good and hot, take one piece of baking paper and flip all the scallops into the pan at the same time. The reason you do it this way is because scallops cook so quickly. If you add them one at a time, the first ones will absorb all the heat from the pan, leaving the subsequent scallops to stew rather than fry and form a beautiful golden ring (or crown) around the white flesh. Sear for 1 minute on each side, then quickly remove. Wait for the pan to get smoking hot again and repeat with the remaining batches.

Place a small scoop of the herb mixture on each of the prepared shells, add a scallop and finish with an extra drizzle of oil. Arrange on a bed of rock salt and serve immediately.

*Pictured on page 118.*

# BAZZA'S SYMI SCHOOL PRAWNS
## WITH GREEK SALAD

My good mate, the one and only Barry Du Bois, always talks about his trips to the Mediterranean. He has been going there and sailing around the islands on his yacht since he was a young man. He came across this dish on the Greek island of Symi and it is his all-time favourite. This recipe is my way of honouring the many times Barry has told me about it – a true legacy of our friendship.

When you make a Greek salad, always serve the feta in big blocks to break up at the table. That way you can divvy it up evenly and make sure everyone gets the same amount of cheese!

sunflower oil, for shallow-frying
3 tablespoons plain flour
2 teaspoons salt flakes
2 teaspoons freshly ground
   black pepper
1 kg small raw prawns, heads
   removed if you like
lemon wedges, to serve

### GREEK SALAD
4 juicy tomatoes, cut into chunks
½ telegraph cucumber, peeled
   in stripes down the length,
   then diced
1 small red onion, finely sliced
185 g (1 cup) Kalamata olives
200 g Greek feta
80 ml (⅓ cup) extra-virgin olive
   oil, plus extra for drizzling
1–2 tablespoons lemon juice or
   sherry vinegar, to taste
2 teaspoons dried Greek oregano
salt flakes and freshly ground
   black pepper
1 green capsicum, cored, deseeded
   and sliced into rings

**SERVES 4-6**

For the Greek salad, place the tomato, cucumber, onion and olives in a large bowl. Crumble in a little of the feta, then halve the rest and put aside. Add the oil, lemon juice or vinegar and oregano, season with salt and pepper and gently toss to combine - don't overmix; this salad is not meant to be handled too much. Place the capsicum on a platter, top with tomato mixture, then the feta slices and finish with an extra drizzle of oil.

Pour sunflower oil into a wide, heavy-based saucepan to a depth of 4 cm and heat over medium–high heat to 180°C.

Place the flour, salt and pepper in a large zip-lock bag. Add the prawns, then seal and shake until they are coated with the seasoned flour.

Test the oil with the handle of a wooden spoon or tip of a prawn tail to see if bubbles appear. Working in batches, grab a handful of prawns, shake off the excess flour mixture and add to the oil. Fry for 2 minutes or until the prawns are pink and crisp. Remove with a slotted spoon and drain on paper towel.

Transfer all the prawns to a platter and serve with lemon wedges and the Greek salad on the side.

*Pictured on page 119.*

# RICE-CRUSTED SARDINES
## WITH AVO ON RYE

Rice is the number-one most important ingredient for a Spanish chef. If you grind it really finely, you'll be amazed at how much texture you can add to your classic sardines on toast. Sardines are a very healthy fish to eat and should be included in your diet as much as possible. We eat them weekly in Spain, as we do anchovies.

50 g Calasparra rice
2 tablespoons plain flour
salt flakes and freshly ground
    black pepper
6 fresh sardines, butterflied (ask
    your fishmonger to do this for you)
olive oil, for pan-frying and
    drizzling
100 g podded edamame beans
100 g canned giant lima beans
    (garrafon) or white beans
½ bunch of flat-leaf parsley, leaves
    picked and finely chopped
2 garlic cloves, minced
1 avocado
lemon wedges, to serve
6 thick slices of rye bread, toasted

**SERVES 6**

Using a small spice grinder or mortar and pestle, grind the rice to a coarse powder. Tip onto a plate.

Whisk together the flour and 2 tablespoons of water in a small bowl to form a smooth batter. Season with salt and pepper.

Pat the sardines dry with paper towel. Dip the skin side only into the batter, then dip both sides into the powdered rice to coat.

Heat 1 tablespoon of oil in a non-stick frying pan over medium heat. Add the sardines, skin-side down, and cook for 4 minutes or until the crust is crisp and golden. Turn and cook for another 30 seconds, then remove and drain on paper towel.

Add the edamame and lima beans, along with a drizzle of oil. Cover and cook over medium heat, stirring occasionally, for 2 minutes or until lightly browned. Stir in the parsley and garlic and season to taste.

Slice the avocado and spread it over the rye toast, then drizzle with oil, squeeze over some lemon juice and sprinkle with salt. Top with the beans and finish with the sardines and a final drizzle of oil. Serve immediately.

# DR CHRIS BROWN'S MISO SALMON

Chris Brown, AKA Gringo, is the healthiest person I know and this is his favourite recipe. He has cooked it for me many, many times. Miso is so easy to use and gives the salmon an amazing umami flavour. My little tip is to wipe the excess miso off the salmon skin before pan-frying to prevent burning. Eat this recipe often enough and I guarantee you'll start to look like Dr Chris!

4 x 180 g salmon fillets, bones removed, skin on
1½ tablespoons white miso paste
1½ tablespoons mirin
1½ tablespoons soy sauce
3 teaspoons sesame oil
1 tablespoon salt flakes
1 tablespoon olive oil
30 g butter, chopped
micro herbs (optional) and garden salad, to serve

## ROAST POTATOES
1 kg desiree potatoes
3 tablespoons olive oil
2 rosemary sprigs, leaves picked
salt flakes

## SERVES 4

Preheat the oven to 200°C (fan-forced). Line a baking tray with baking paper.

For the roast potatoes, cut the unpeeled potatoes into quarters or thumb-sized chunks. Place in a saucepan of cold water and bring to the boil, then cook for 10–15 minutes until almost tender. Drain and shake to rough them up a bit, then spread over the prepared tray and roast for 10 minutes without any oil. Remove the tray from the oven, coat the potatoes with the oil, rosemary and salt and toss to coat. Spread over the tray again and roast for a further 20–30 minutes or until crisp and golden.

Meanwhile, pat the salmon fillets dry with paper towel and score the skin with a sharp knife.

Combine the miso, mirin, soy sauce, sesame oil and salt in a shallow dish. Add the salmon and turn to coat in the marinade, then set aside for 15 minutes to marinate.

When the potatoes are almost ready, remove the salmon from the marinade and pat dry. Heat the oil in a large frying pan over medium heat, add the fish, skin-side down, and press with an egg flip to ensure the skin has maximum contact with the pan and to prevent it from curling up. If the pan gets too hot the skin will burn before the flesh is cooked, so keep it at medium.

Keep the fish skin-side down for 90 per cent of the cooking time, basting regularly with the pan juices. As the fillets cook, the sides will change from orange to pink. Cook for 2–3 minutes, until the pink reaches three-quarters of the way up the side, then add the butter and flip the fillets over. Cook for another 30 seconds, basting with the butter, then remove from the heat.

Divide the salmon and roast potatoes among plates, garnish with micro herbs, if using, and serve with a crisp salad.

# CRISPY SKINNED BARRAMUNDI
## WITH CHERRY TOMATOES & FENNEL

There is nothing more Australian than barramundi on a barbecue so, cliché or not, I had to include this dish in my cookbook. Barramundi is the most beloved fish of Indigenous Australians and it is widely available year round, both freshwater and saltwater varieties.

I use a bed of cherry tomatoes to cook the barramundi perfectly, grilling the skin and then flipping the fish onto the tomatoes so that the flesh never directly touches the barbecue plate. The tomatoes blister and take on some of the lovely barra flavour and the fish essentially steams on top.

2 x 250 g barramundi fillets,
  bones removed, skin on
salt flakes
30 g butter
250 g cherry tomatoes on the vine

**SALAD**
250 g mixed heirloom cherry
  tomatoes, quartered
1 tablespoon large capers
4 wedges of preserved lemon rind,
  finely sliced
50 g (⅓ cup) sun-dried tomatoes,
  roughly torn
10 black olives
2 tablespoons soft Persian feta
1 baby cos lettuce, leaves
  separated and washed
½ fennel bulb, trimmed and finely
  sliced on a mandoline
salt flakes and freshly ground
  black pepper
generous drizzle of extra-virgin
  olive oil

**SERVES 2**

Pat the barramundi fillets dry with paper towel and score the skin with a sharp knife at least five times. Season each fillet with 2 teaspoons of salt and rub into the skin.

Preheat a barbecue hot plate to high, add the butter and let it melt. Add the fillets, skin-side down, and cook without turning for at least 8 minutes to ensure crispy skin, pushing down constantly so they don't curl up. At the same time, cook the tomatoes on the hot plate until soft and beginning to blister.

When the fillets are crispy skinned, lift them off the hot plate and put them on top of the tomatoes, flesh-side down (you don't want the fleshy underside to come into contact with the hot plate at all). Cook for a further 3 minutes.

Meanwhile, to make the salad, gently toss together all the ingredients in a bowl.

Serve the fish and charred tomatoes with the salad.

# PRAWN POPCORN LETTUCE CUPS

Lettuce cups are such a healthy and refreshing snack or starter. The light tempura batter gives the prawns great texture and works perfectly with the Asian flavours in the dressing. Make sure you soak the lettuce cups in iced water for plenty of time so they are really cold and crispy. For maximum crunch, drain the prawns on paper towel after frying to soak up any excess oil. This is the perfect entrée; you can't go wrong.

200 g rice vermicelli noodles
250 ml (1 cup) vegetable oil
500 g fresh prawn meat, chopped
  into 1.5 cm pieces
250 g rice flour
1 iceberg lettuce, leaves separated
  into 'cups'

**GINGER DRESSING**
3 tablespoons hoisin sauce
2 tablespoons light soy sauce
2 tablespoons sweet chilli sauce
juice of 1 lime
1 tablespoon grated ginger
1 hot chilli, finely chopped
  (optional, if you want to turn
  up the heat!)

**SALAD**
½ bunch of mint, leaves picked
½ bunch of coriander, leaves
  picked
100 g soy bean sprouts
100 g purple cabbage, shredded
60 g toasted salted cashews,
  chopped
1 Lebanese cucumber,
  finely chopped

**TEMPURA BATTER**
200 g tempura flour
300 ml cold soda water

**SERVES 4**

To make the ginger dressing, mix together all the ingredients in a small bowl.

Combine all the salad ingredients in a large bowl.

Place the noodles in a heatproof bowl, cover with boiling water and stand for 5 minutes or until tender. Rinse with cold water, then drain and set aside.

For the tempura batter, whisk together the flour and soda water with a fork until well combined. Don't worry about the lumps.

Heat the oil in a wok or deep frying pan over high heat until it's smoking hot. Lightly dust the prawn pieces in rice flour, then place in a sieve and shake off the excess. Dip the prawn pieces into the cold tempura batter until completely coated.

Working in batches, deep-fry the battered prawn pieces until they are a light popcorn colour and wonderfully crunchy. This should only take 1 minute or so. Remove and shake off any excess oil, then drain on paper towel.

Just before serving, combine the salad and noodles and toss through the dressing.

Divide the prawn popcorn, noodles and salad among lettuce cups and serve.

# KINGFISH CEVICHE

This is one of my favourite recipes. I was taught how to make it by Diego Muñoz, head chef at Astrid y Gaston, a Peruvian restaurant that is one of the best in the world. I was lucky enough to work with Diego for a time at Tony Bilson's bistro in Sydney.

Invented in Peru, ceviche is like the sashimi of South American cuisine. The raw fish is cooked by citrus rather than heat. This is a very authentic way to make it; it is vivacious and explosive, like someone giving you a kiss and then slapping you in the face! The intense spiciness of the fish is balanced out by the gentle sweet potato, and then the vodka chaser … wow. So many feelings in such a short space of time! I've made this at many of my live cooking shows and the expression on people's faces when they try it is priceless. This is the kind of food you remember.

1 tablespoon extra-virgin olive oil
1 small celery stick, roughly chopped
1 long red chilli, roughly chopped
1 garlic clove, roughly chopped
1 cm piece of ginger, peeled and roughly chopped
½ bunch of coriander, leaves and stems picked, plus extra to serve
juice of 2 lemons
juice of 1 lime
400 g sashimi-grade kingfish fillet, cut into 1 cm slices
½ red onion, finely sliced
1 ice cube
2 shots of vodka

## POACHED SWEET POTATO
200 g caster sugar
1 star anise
1 sweet potato (about 250 g), peeled and cut into 1 cm dice
juice of ½ lime

**SERVES 2 (OR 4 AS A STARTER)**

To make the poached sweet potato, place the sugar and star anise in a small saucepan, add 200 ml of water and stir over low heat until the sugar has dissolved. Add the sweet potato and simmer gently for 10 minutes (maximum) or until just tender. Drain and place in a bowl, then drizzle with the lime juice and set aside to cool.

Meanwhile, place the oil, celery, chilli, garlic, ginger, coriander leaves and stems and lemon and lime juice in a small food processor and blend until smooth. Pour into a serving bowl.

Add the kingfish, onion and ice cube to the bowl and gently toss to coat. Stand for 4 minutes – during this time the acid from the citrus will 'cook' the protein in the fish.

Pour the vodka into two shot glasses and add a splash of the citrus juice from the fish. Serve with the ceviche and poached sweet potato, with the extra coriander leaves scattered over the top.

# HOT SMOKED SALMON
## WITH HORSERADISH CREAM & HOMEMADE LAVOSH

I always make this when I'm entertaining at home as it's such a great dish to have in the middle of the table for people to enjoy DIY-style. It's also very easy to pre-prepare.

If you don't have a smoker, you can buy little boxes of smoking chips from any hardware store and pop them in the barbecue with the hood closed. It's very easy to do. Don't be scared of using too much marinade on your salmon as the flavours will really work with the smokiness. And if you can get fresh horseradish or wasabi … wow. This is a real family favourite.

1 side of skinless salmon
  (about 1.2 kg)
extra-virgin olive oil, for brushing
salt flakes and freshly ground
  black pepper
finely grated zest of 1 lemon
finely grated zest of 1 lime
2 dried chillies, crumbled
12 rosemary, lemon thyme and
  marjoram sprigs (4 of each),
  leaves picked and chopped
3 cups woodchips, such as mesquite
  or hickory, soaked in water for
  at least an hour, drained
lemon leaves on branches or
  1 bunch of rosemary
8 dill sprigs, to serve

### LAVOSH CRACKERS
100 g (1 cup) rye flour
300 g (2 cups) plain flour,
  plus extra for dusting
1 tablespoon salt flakes,
  plus extra for sprinkling
100 ml extra-virgin olive oil,
  plus extra for drizzling

### HORSERADISH CREAM
200 g creme fraiche
50 g finely grated fresh
  horseradish, or to taste (see Tip)
salt flakes and freshly ground
  black pepper

**SERVES 4–6 AS A STARTER**

To make the lavosh crackers, preheat the oven to 250°C (fan-forced). Line three large baking trays with baking paper.

Sift the flours into the bowl of a stand mixer fitted with the dough hook and add the salt. Make a well in the centre, add the oil and 200 ml of water and knead briefly (just a minute or two until the dough comes together). Turn it out onto a lightly floured surface and divide into four even portions. Roll each portion out as thin as possible (or run them through a pasta machine).

Cut into sheets to fit the prepared trays, then drizzle with extra oil, sprinkle with extra salt and bake in batches for 10 minutes. Allow to cool, then break into pieces and store in an airtight container for 3–4 days.

To make the horseradish cream, simply combine all the ingredients in a bowl. Taste and adjust the seasoning if needed, then refrigerate until required.

For the hot smoked salmon, brush the salmon with oil and season to taste, then rub the lemon and lime zest, chilli and chopped herbs over the salmon. Place on a baking tray and set aside.

Preheat a coal-bedded kettle barbecue until the coals turn white, then add the soaked woodchips and lemon leaves or rosemary to the coals. When they start to smoke, place the salmon on an oiled rack in the barbecue, then cover and smoke for 20–25 minutes until cooked through. Remove and set aside until cool enough to handle. It's now ready to eat or you can store it in an airtight container in the fridge for up to 3 days and serve it chilled.

Roughly flake the flesh, discarding the bones, and garnish with the dill sprigs. Serve with the horseradish cream and lavosh crackers.

**TIP**

If you don't have fresh horseradish, use wasabi paste instead. Add it gradually and taste as you go.

CHICKEN

# CRISPY CHICKEN BURGERS

I love this recipe, which was inspired by my visit to Yeastie Boys Bagels in LA (one of the coolest food trucks around). Their chicken burger always sold out, which is a solid tick of approval from American fried-chicken pros. The density of the bagel makes the crispy chicken lighter, and that hole in the middle means you eat less bread! How good is that? If the bagel is too dense, put the burger in a sandwich press so it warms through and softens slightly.

Make sure you load it with a lot of sauce, and be prepared: you need to have a big mouth for the first bite – works for me!

4 bagels, bread rolls or brioche
  buns, toasted if preferred
Japanese mayonnaise (kewpie),
  for spreading
sriracha chilli sauce, for spreading
  (optional)
finely sliced tomato, red onion and
  cucumber, to serve
freshly ground black pepper

**CRISPY FRIED CHICKEN**
750 g chicken breast fillets
pinch of salt flakes
pinch of dried rosemary
pinch of ground turmeric
pinch of dried oregano
pinch of crushed black peppercorns
6 cm piece of ginger, peeled and
  finely grated
2 garlic cloves, finely grated
finely grated zest of 1 lemon
1 egg
2 tablespoons plain flour
200 g (3 ⅓ cups) panko
  breadcrumbs
large handful of rolled oats
vegetable oil, for deep-frying

**SERVES 4**

To prepare the crispy fried chicken, place the chicken fillets in a zip-lock bag, add the salt, rosemary, turmeric, oregano and crushed peppercorns and shake until the chicken is well coated. Add the grated ginger, garlic and lemon zest and shake the bag again to coat. Crack the egg into the bag, add the flour and shake again.

In a separate bag, combine the breadcrumbs and oats.

Working with one fillet at a time, add the chicken to the breadcrumb mixture and shake to apply a final coat. Don't do this in the original bag or everything will stick together.

Heat the oil for deep-frying in a large heavy-based saucepan (or deep-fryer) over high heat and heat to 180°C. Add the chicken and cook for 5 minutes or until cooked through and golden brown on both sides. Remove and drain on paper towel. When cool enough to handle, carve each breast on an angle into three or four thick slices.

Cut the bagels or buns in half and spread both halves with mayo and sriracha, if using. Layer the tomato and onion on the bottom slice. Add two slices of crispy fried chicken and top with the cucumber, some black pepper and the bagel or bun lids.

# MISO CHICKEN BOWL

These vibrant, colourful bowls are so on trend in Australia. This one uses a one-tray wonder miso chicken that is very easy to make. While it's in the oven you can work on the veggies, making them all different shapes for maximum texture. I love to use as wide a variety of condiments as possible with this, such as seaweed chips, wasabi peas and kewpie mayo with sriracha.

600 g chicken thigh fillets
juice of 1 lime
450 g packet microwave brown rice
½ baby Chinese cabbage
   (wombok), very finely sliced
¼ red cabbage, very finely sliced
310 g (2 cups) shredded carrot
1 large telegraph cucumber, peeled
   lengthways into ribbons
1 large avocado, sliced
¼ bunch of coriander, leaves
   picked and chopped
3 tablespoons sesame seeds,
   toasted

## MARINADE
1 ½ tablespoons white miso paste
2 cm piece of ginger, peeled
   and grated
2 teaspoons honey
1 ½ tablespoons extra-virgin
   olive oil
1 ½ tablespoons rice wine vinegar
1 ½ tablespoons soy sauce

## OPTIONAL GARNISHES
wasabi peas, crispy fried shallots,
crispy seaweed chips, sriracha
mayonnaise, sweet chilli sauce
and extra lime wedges

**SERVES 4–6**

Preheat the oven to 220°C (fan-forced). Line a baking tray with baking paper.

To make the marinade, combine all the ingredients in a jug and whisk with a fork until smooth.

Place the chicken in a bowl, add half the marinade and toss to coat. Arrange the chicken on the prepared tray in a single layer and bake for 20 minutes or until golden and cooked through. Finely slice the chicken.

Stir the lime juice through the remaining marinade and set aside. This will be your dressing.

Heat the rice according to the packet instructions. Toss together the rice, Chinese cabbage and half the miso dressing.

To serve, divide the rice mixture evenly among bowls and add the chicken, red cabbage, carrot, cucumber, avocado and coriander. Sprinkle with the sesame seeds and drizzle over the remaining dressing. Serve with any, all or none of the optional garnishes.

# MY THAI GREEN CURRY
## FROM SCRATCH

Most people buy a pre-made paste when making curry, but one day you should really try making the real deal like this – the aromas and fragrance are insane. Try to use a mortar and pestle, too, as the stone grinding does something amazing to the ingredients. The most important step in this recipe is caramelising the paste – you need to take it really far to truly meld the flavours.

I've used the traditional small Thai eggplants here, but you can sub in any veggies you like. Don't be scared of the chillies – I like my green curry really hot as it's meant to be!

2 tablespoons coconut oil
1 tablespoon fish sauce
1 teaspoon palm sugar
750 ml (3 cups) coconut cream
250 ml (1 cup) chicken stock, plus extra if needed
5 chicken thigh fillets, skin on, finely sliced
5 Thai eggplants, quartered
1 bunch of Thai basil, leaves picked, to serve
steamed rice, to serve

**CURRY PASTE**
4 large green chillies, halved, deseeded and chopped
2 bird's eye chillies, halved, deseeded and chopped
4 golden shallots
strips of peel from 1 makrut lime
2 makrut lime leaves
6 cm piece of turmeric, peeled and roughly chopped
6 cm piece of galangal, peeled and roughly chopped
6 garlic cloves, peeled
1 lemongrass stalk, white part only, roughly chopped
1 bunch of coriander, leaves picked (save for garnish), roots well washed
1 teaspoon coriander seeds, toasted
1 teaspoon white peppercorns
1 teaspoon ground cumin
1 teaspoon shrimp paste

**SERVES 4**

To make the curry paste, pound the chilli, shallot, makrut lime peel and leaves, turmeric, galangal, garlic and lemongrass using a mortar and pestle. Add the coriander root and continue pounding to a paste. (Don't add the coriander leaves now or they will bruise and turn your curry black.) Add the coriander seeds, white peppercorns, cumin and shrimp paste and pound together. (You could also use a food processor to make the paste if preferred.)

Melt the coconut oil in a large saucepan over medium heat, then reduce the heat to low and add the paste. Cook, stirring, for about 6 minutes until the paste caramelises. This step is really important as it mellows and sweetens the raw ingredients.

Season with the fish sauce and palm sugar, then add the coconut cream and stir well. Add the chicken stock and bring to a simmer, then add the chicken and eggplant and cook over medium heat for 8 minutes or until the chicken is cooked through. If it's too dry, add another little splash of stock or water. Don't let it boil or the chicken will become tough.

Scatter with the coriander and basil leaves and serve with steamed rice.

# ROAST CHICKEN

Every cookbook has a recipe for the perfect roast chicken and this is mine. My secret is to use mushrooms under the skin. Mushrooms have a really high moisture content, so when placed under the skin with plenty of butter they keep the bird incredibly moist and succulent. You also need to fill the cavity all the way to the top, as roast chickens dry from the inside out.

With all the veggies cooked in the same tray, when the chicken comes out of the oven, that's dinner done! Make sure you get some special veggies like heirloom carrots or little beetroots – it's really worth it. I hope this will become your go-to roast chicken recipe.

20 g unsalted butter, softened
400 g swiss brown mushrooms, quartered
3 thyme sprigs, leaves picked
salt flakes and freshly ground black pepper
1 large (about 2.5 kg) chicken
1 teaspoon smoked paprika
2 portobello mushrooms

**STUFFING**
1 tablespoon olive oil
2 chorizo sausages, finely diced
4 flat mushrooms, finely chopped
4 spring onions, white and green parts finely chopped
salt flakes and freshly ground black pepper

**ROASTED VEGETABLES**
1 bunch of baby beets (golden and purple), scrubbed and halved
1 bunch of baby carrots (purple, yellow, orange), scrubbed and trimmed
1 bunch of spring onions, trimmed
2 baby fennel bulbs, trimmed and quartered
salt flakes and freshly ground black pepper
olive oil, for drizzling

**SERVES 4–6**

Preheat the oven to 180°C (fan-forced).

Blend the butter, mushrooms and thyme in a food processor and season generously with salt and pepper.

Gently loosen the skin on the chicken by pushing your fingers along the surface of the meat around the breast and thighs. Push the butter mixture under the skin, being careful not to tear it, and work it as far down under the skin as possible. Sprinkle the paprika over the bird and rub until evenly coated.

For the stuffing, heat the oil in a large frying pan over medium–high heat, add the chorizo, mushroom and spring onion and cook, stirring regularly, for 2 minutes. Season to taste with salt and pepper and remove from the heat.

Push one of the portobello mushrooms into the chicken cavity, then add the stuffing, pressing it in firmly. Seal the cavity with the other mushroom.

For the roasted vegetables, place the prepared veggies in a large roasting tin. Season generously with salt and pepper, then drizzle with oil and mix together well with your hands. Spread out in a single layer and place the chicken on top. Roast for 1 hour 10 minutes or until the meat is cooked through and the vegetables are tender and caramelised.

Remove the chicken and rest for 5 minutes. Carve and serve with the roasted vegetables and the stuffing.

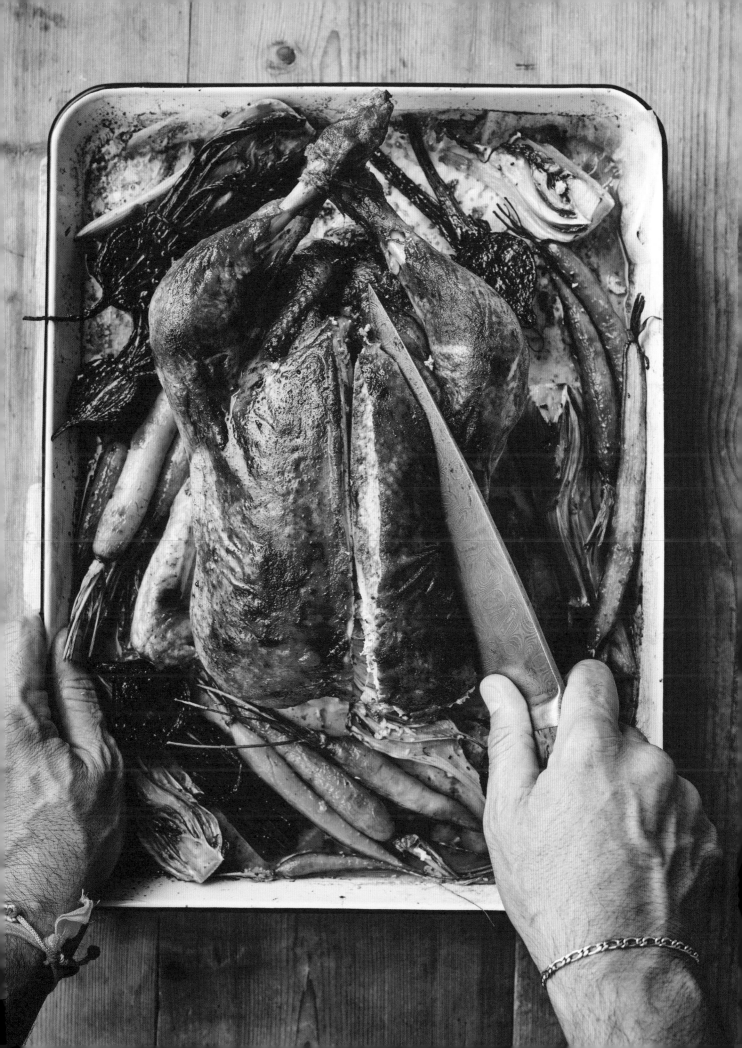

Crispy Chicken Schnitzy with Buttery Centre & Perfect Mash, see page 146
Chicken & Chorizo Ballotine, see page 147

# CRISPY CHICKEN SCHNITZY
## WITH BUTTERY CENTRE & PERFECT MASH

Chicken schnitzels can easily dry out during the cooking process. This technique of putting butter inside like a kiev is the best way to keep them nice and moist.

3 large chicken breast fillets
salt flakes and freshly ground
   black pepper
1 tablespoon smoked paprika
150 g (1 cup) plain flour
120 g (2 cups) panko breadcrumbs
3 eggs
light olive oil, for shallow-frying

### PERFECT MASH
rock salt, for roasting
1 kg even-sized large dutch cream
   potatoes, unpeeled, scrubbed
250 ml (1 cup) pouring cream
100 g butter, at room temperature
salt flakes

### GARLIC BUTTER
100 g butter, at room temperature
juice of ¼ lemon
4 garlic cloves
½ bunch of chives
salt flakes and freshly ground
   black pepper

**SERVES 6**

**TIP**

This is delicious served with the tomato and burrata salad on page 64.

To make the mash, preheat the oven to 200°C (fan-forced). Make a solid bed of rock salt on the base of a roasting tin, then sit the potatoes on top. (This will stop the potatoes rolling around and also help draw out the moisture.) Roast for 1½–2 hours until dry and wrinkled.

Using a tea towel to hold the hot potatoes, cut them in half lengthways with a serrated knife and scoop out the flesh. Working in batches, pass the flesh through a mouli or a potato ricer into a large non-stick frying pan.

Meanwhile, combine the cream and butter in a small saucepan over medium–high heat and bring almost to the boil. Remove from the heat.

Stir the potato over low heat for 1 minute to remove the last of the moisture, then remove from the heat. Gradually add the cream and butter mixture, beating with a strong whisk until the mash is smooth and fluffy. Season generously with salt flakes.

Meanwhile, to prepare the garlic butter, place all the ingredients in a small food processor and pulse to a smooth paste. Set aside.

Slice each chicken breast lengthways into two even halves. Using a smaller knife, cut a little pocket widthways into each half, as deep as you can without cutting all the way through.

Place a large tablespoon of the garlic butter into each pocket and flatten with your hand, spreading it internally as much as possible. Keep the pocket closed using the butter as glue. Season each breast with salt, pepper and paprika, then chill in the fridge for 10 minutes or so.

Tip the flour into a shallow bowl, the breadcrumbs into a second bowl, and lightly beat the eggs in a third.

Dredge each breast first in the flour, shaking off any excess, then dip into the egg, allowing any excess to drip off. Dunk into the breadcrumbs, pressing to make sure each breast is fully covered and evenly coated.

Pour the oil into a large frying pan to a depth of 1 cm and over very high heat. Working in two batches, cook the crumbed chicken for 3–5 minutes on each side until golden brown and cooked through. Remove and rest on paper towel for 2 minutes, then serve with the mash and a fresh salad.

*Pictured on page 145.*

# CHICKEN & CHORIZO BALLOTINE

This dish is a great way to give humble chicken thighs restaurant-quality presentation. When rolling the chicken with the foil, make sure it is very tight and there are no perforations, so that no water gets in to dry out the chicken during the poaching process. The filling is very easy to make and the chorizo brings so much flavour. Panko breadcrumbs – freeze-dried Japanese white breadcrumbs – are the best as they don't absorb as much oil as other varieties so stay nice and crunchy. They're worth every penny!

3 large chicken thigh fillets, skin on
8 thin slices of jamon or pancetta
2 chorizo sausages
2 field mushrooms, halved
40 g butter
chopped chives, to serve

**WHITE BEAN SALAD**
400 g canned white beans,
　drained and rinsed
1 red chilli, deseeded and
　finely diced
1 golden shallot, finely diced
1 bunch of chives, finely chopped
2 tablespoons Manzanilla olives,
　roughly chopped
3 tablespoons Japanese
　mayonnaise (kewpie)
salt flakes and freshly ground
　black pepper

**SERVES 4**

The white bean salad can be made with canned chickpeas instead, if you prefer.

Preheat the oven 200°C (fan-forced).

Using a meat cleaver or rolling pin, flatten the thicker parts of the chicken fillets. Don't overdo it – you just want to give them a more uniform thickness.

Place a large sheet of foil on your bench and top with a sheet of baking paper. Place the jamon or pancetta on the paper, slightly overlapping the slices, then arrange the chicken on top in a single layer, without overlapping.

Puree the chorizo and mushroom in a food processor, then spread the mixture evenly down the length of the chicken, leaving a thin border on the edges. Using the foil and paper to help you, roll the chicken into a tight cylinder. Pinch and twist the ends like a lolly wrapper so the parcel is completely sealed. It's very important that no water can get in during poaching so if you are in any doubt at all, add another layer of foil and twist very tightly to make sure it's properly sealed.

Bring a medium saucepan of water to the boil. Reduce to a simmer, add the chicken parcel and poach gently for 25–30 minutes or until just cooked through and firm to the touch.

Remove from the pan and take off the foil and paper wrapping. Melt the butter in a large frying pan over high heat and pan-fry the chicken so the jamon or pancetta is nice and crispy, basting regularly with the butter. Leave to rest in the pan while you make the salad.

To make the white bean salad, combine all the ingredients in a bowl. Taste and adjust the seasoning if needed.

Cut the chicken ballotine into 3–4 cm thick slices and serve with the white bean salad, finished with a sprinkling of chives.

*Pictured on page 144.*

# MAMA'S CHICKEN SOUP

This is what we cook in the Maestre house when someone needs a big culinary hug. If you've had a hard day or you're not feeling well, Mama's home cooking will make everything better. This is about nourishing the soul, not just the belly.

This is a great soup base so you can get creative with the flavours and finishes – I've given you a few different combinations to try below. If you're following the original recipe, make sure you only add the egg right at the end so it doesn't overcook. You want to be able to crack it and release the runny yolk.

3 tablespoons extra-virgin olive oil
4 onions, diced
2 leeks, 2 cm trimmed off the top, well washed and diced
1 head of garlic, halved horizontally
1/3 bunch of thyme, leaves picked
4 bay leaves
1 chicken (about 1.2 kg)
2 litres boiling water
1/2 bunch of celery, roughly chopped (save the leaves and finely chop for garnish)
4 carrots, roughly chopped
500 g macaroni or other small pasta shape
salt flakes and freshly ground black pepper
4–6 eggs

SERVES 4–6

Heat the oil in a large saucepan over medium heat, add the onion, leek, garlic, thyme and bay leaves and cook, stirring regularly, for about 6 minutes until softened without taking on colour. Add the chicken, then pour in the boiling water straight from the kettle. Bring to the boil, then reduce the heat and simmer for 45 minutes.

Add the celery and carrot and cook for a further 5 minutes, then remove the chicken and place on a tray.

Add the pasta to the soup and cook for another 8 minutes or until al dente. Season with salt and pepper. Carefully crack the eggs into the pan and poach for 3 minutes or until cooked to your liking.

Portion out the chicken breasts, legs and wings. Place two pieces of chicken and one poached egg in each bowl, then ladle over the stock and vegetables. Garnish with the reserved celery leaves and serve.

## VARIATIONS

- For a Chinese-style chicken soup, you can add soy sauce, sesame oil and chilli sauce and replace the pasta with noodles.
- Omit the eggs and pasta and add a splash of cream and some canned corn for a creamy chicken and corn soup.
- Replace the eggs and pasta with grilled chorizo and chickpeas for a Spanish-style chicken and chorizo broth.
- For a chicken minestrone, omit the eggs and swap the pasta for canned giant lima beans (garrafon) or white beans. Add passata and dried oregano, and serve with chopped basil and grated parmesan.

# BARBECUED GARLIC CHICKEN
## WITH CAULIFLOWER TABBOULEH

Feel free to use any woody herbs you have handy – you want these hardier herbs as they will hold up better to the heat of the barbecue. Grating the cauliflower and broccoli for the tabbouleh gives this salad a new dimension and makes it super healthy.

1 large chicken (about 2.5 kg)
salt flakes
125 g (½ cup) Greek yoghurt
sprinkling of ground sumac, to serve

### GARLIC MARINADE
2 heads of garlic, cloves separated
  and peeled
3 tablespoons extra-virgin olive oil
½ bunch of lemon thyme, leaves
  picked
½ bunch of thyme, leaves picked
½ bunch of sage, leaves picked
3 rosemary sprigs, leaves picked
2 oregano sprigs, leaves picked

### TABBOULEH
½ small head of cauliflower, grated
½ small head of broccoli, grated
100 g cherry tomatoes, quartered
½ small red onion, diced
1 small zucchini, diced
1 bunch of flat-leaf parsley, leaves
  picked and finely chopped
1 bunch of coriander, leaves picked
  and finely chopped
1 bunch of basil, leaves picked and
  finely chopped
80 ml (⅓ cup) extra-virgin
  olive oil
juice of 1 lemon
1 tablespoon ground sumac
salt flakes and freshly ground
  black pepper

**SERVES 6–8**

Preheat the barbecue to high.

To make the marinade, grind the garlic using a large mortar and pestle, gradually adding the olive oil to form a paste. Add the herbs to the mortar and grind until the mixture resembles a garlic butter. (You could also use a food processor if that's easier.)

Next, spatchcock the chicken. To do this, place the chicken on a board, breast-side down, with the legs facing towards you. Using kitchen scissors, cut through the rib bones along each side of the parson's nose and backbone, then remove the backbone. Open the chicken out flat and flip it over. Use the heel of your hand to flatten the breastbone until the meat is all one thickness.

Place the bird, bone-side down, on the board and score with deep cuts all over using a chef's knife. This will help the flavours in the marinade infuse into the meat, and also means it will cook more quickly. Rub the garlic marinade over the top of the chicken, and into the incisions.

Place the chicken, bone-side down, on the barbecue and turn the heat down to medium–high. Season well with salt. Cover the barbecue and leave the chicken to cook for about 1 hour 10 minutes. There is no need to flip it over, as the barbecue will steam the top until it is cooked through. This also stops the garlic marinade coming into direct contact with the hot plate, so it won't burn and develop a bitter flavour.

While the chicken is cooking, prepare the tabbouleh. Combine the vegetables and herbs in a large bowl, dress with the oil, lemon juice and sumac, and season with salt and pepper. Toss together well.

When the chicken is cooked and the meat starts to come away from the bone, remove it from the barbecue and cut into pieces. Serve with the tabbouleh and Greek yoghurt, and finish with a sprinkling of sumac.

# MEAT

# EASY PORK SAN CHOY BAU

Lettuce cups are a big favourite in our house. I cook this dish all the time as my kids love it. It's playful and simple, with lovely Asian flavours.

Iceberg lettuce is very cheap and gives you so much bang for your buck. I use pork tenderloin instead of mince because I find it a bit easier to eat, but you can swap it for pork mince if you want to. I always add a lot of crunchy noodles for texture.

1 tablespoon extra-virgin olive oil
1 small onion, finely chopped
500 g pork tenderloins, finely sliced
    (or use pork mince)
4 garlic cloves, crushed
220 g canned water chestnuts,
    drained and chopped
125 g canned corn kernels, drained
2 tablespoons oyster sauce
1 tablespoon hoisin sauce
1 tablespoon dark soy sauce
1 teaspoon sesame oil
2 handfuls of crunchy fried noodles
5 spring onions, trimmed and
    finely sliced
½ bunch of coriander, leaves
    picked and chopped
12 iceberg lettuce leaves,
    separated and washed

**SERVES 4**

Heat the oil in a medium frying pan over high heat, add the onion and cook for a few minutes until softened. Add the pork and stir-fry for 3–4 minutes until browned and cooked through. (If you use mince, break up any large chunks with the back of your wooden spoon as you go.) Add the garlic, water chestnut and corn and cook, stirring, for another minute or two.

Stir in the oyster sauce, hoisin, dark soy and sesame oil and cook until the sauce has thickened slightly.

Remove the pan from the heat and stir through the noodles, spring onion and coriander leaves.

Spoon the mixture into the lettuce cups and serve.

*Perfect Pork Belly with Waldorf Salad, see page 158*

# PERFECT PORK BELLY
## WITH WALDORF SALAD

Pork belly is the only part of the pig that gives you everything: fat, crunch and flesh. You just have to be smart with how you cook it. The secret is to score the skin and allow it to dry out overnight in the fridge to get the crackle really nice and crisp. Pre-frying the skin helps, too. But for me, the game changer is very carefully adding the stock to the tray without allowing any of it to touch the skin, otherwise you'll undo all your good work. This roast pork is great in sandwiches, wraps and tacos, so don't be afraid to cook a big portion for maximum leftover goodness.

1.2 kg pork belly
salt flakes and freshly ground
    black pepper
olive oil, for pan-frying
2 fennel bulbs, trimmed and
    roughly chopped
5 thyme sprigs
2 heads of garlic, halved
    horizontally, skin left on
6 star anise
2 tablespoons fennel seeds
1 tablespoon smoked paprika
300 ml white wine (preferably
    chardonnay as it has a
    nutty flavour)
500 ml (2 cups) chicken stock
1 tablespoon dijon or
    wholegrain mustard
1 tablespoon horseradish cream
freshly grated horseradish or
    wasabi, to serve

### CANDIED WALNUTS
200 g (2 cups) walnuts
3 tablespoons caster sugar
pinch of dried chilli flakes

### WALDORF SALAD
2 small green apples
2 tablespoons lemon juice
3 tablespoons whole-egg
    mayonnaise
salt flakes and freshly ground
    black pepper
2 little gem or baby cos lettuce
6 inner celery sticks, including
    leaves, finely sliced (about 1 cup)

**SERVES 6**

Preheat the oven to 180°C (fan-forced) for at least 30 minutes to ensure it is nice and hot. Take the pork out of the fridge and bring it to room temperature.

Meanwhile, to make the candied walnuts, line a baking tray with baking paper. Toast the walnuts in a large frying pan over medium heat until lightly golden. Sprinkle over the sugar and chilli flakes and cook, shaking the pan, until the sugar has dissolved and caramelised. Transfer to the prepared tray and leave to cool for 10–15 minutes.

Using a sharp knife or Stanley knife, cut shallow incisions in the pork belly skin in a criss-cross pattern (similar to calamari). Season the skin generously with salt and rub it in with your hands, making sure it gets into the incisions. Using your hands will also help to bring the meat to room temperature, which will help with the cooking process. Season with black pepper.

Heat a good splash of oil a large flameproof roasting tin over medium heat, add the fennel, thyme sprigs, garlic heads, star anise and 1 tablespoon of fennel seeds and cook for about 3 minutes until aromatic.

Push the fennel mixture to the outer edges of the tin, leaving a space for the pork in the middle. Add the pork belly, skin-side down, and press on it with your hands and sear for 5–7 minutes until golden brown. Take your time to get it nice and golden as this will ensure a crisp crackling.

Turn the pork over so it is skin-side up and rub with the paprika and remaining fennel seeds. Carefully pour the wine into the tin without touching the pork skin and stir to scrape up any bits caught on the base. Cook off the alcohol for a few minutes and bring to the boil (don't skip this step or the alcoholic flavour will be too strong). Add enough stock to come just below the skin and bring back to the boil. Don't allow the pork skin to get wet or you won't get that all-important crispy crackling.

Carefully transfer the tin to the oven, making sure it is still bubbling from the boil, and roast for 2½–3 hours until the meat is very tender and the crackling is irresistible.

Meanwhile, to make the salad, finely slice the apples using a mandoline or a sharp knife. Place in a bowl with 1 tablespoon of the lemon juice and toss to coat. Place the mayonnaise, remaining lemon juice and 1 tablespoon of water in a screw-top jar, season with salt and pepper and shake to combine. Trim the lettuce and separate the leaves. Place in a large, shallow bowl and scatter with the celery, apple and candied walnuts.

Remove the pork belly from the tin and rest on a large platter or board – don't cover it with anything. Strain the pan juices into a saucepan, discarding the solids, and stir in the mustard and horseradish cream. Pour into a jug.

Using a bread knife, carve the pork belly into chunky slices. Top with the freshly grated horseradish or wasabi and serve with the waldorf salad and the sauce alongside.

*Pictured on pages 156–157.*

TIP

For a more relaxed version of this dish, slice all of the pork and divide it among 12 split bread rolls. Add the salad and serve them as sliders.

# STICKY MUSTARD PORK RIBS
## WITH COLESLAW

Pork ribs are my favourite because they cook faster than beef and don't dry out as quickly as lamb. For perfect ribs, make sure you cook them from room temperature rather than cold from the fridge. Sear and brown them very well all over before braising to get that lovely crispy edge on the flesh, and make sure to glaze them generously when it comes time to barbecue. In the unlikely event of leftovers, always pull the meat off the bones before storing it in the fridge. The leftover meat is great for a quick stir-fry or pulled pork sandwiches.

2 tablespoons olive oil
2 kg American-style pork ribs
salt flakes
2 litres chicken stock, plus extra
    if needed
175 g wholegrain mustard
1 tablespoon dijon mustard
3 tablespoons brown sugar
25 g butter
1 tablespoon fennel seeds, ground
6 cm piece of ginger, peeled and
    finely chopped
2 tablespoons brown vinegar
1 tablespoon Worcestershire sauce

### COLESLAW
½ small red cabbage, shredded
¼ white cabbage, shredded
2 carrots, peeled and cut into
    fine matchsticks
1 small onion, halved and
    finely sliced
2 teaspoons horseradish cream
125 g (½ cup) My Quick Aioli
    (see page 29)
1 tablespoon lemon juice
1 tablespoon extra-virgin olive oil
1 tablespoon dijon mustard
salt flakes and freshly ground
    black pepper

**SERVES 4**

Preheat your barbecue hot plate to high and add the oil. Season the pork ribs with salt, then brown for 2–3 minutes on each side or until golden. Set aside.

Combine the stock, mustards, sugar, butter, fennel seeds and ginger in a large saucepan and bring to the boil over high heat. Reduce the heat to medium, add the pork ribs, then braise for 2–3 hours, making sure they are immersed in the liquid at all times. Add a splash more stock or water if needed.

Remove the ribs from the braising liquid and rest on a board. Increase the heat to high and boil the liquid for 20–30 minutes until it has reduced to 160 ml (⅔ cup). Add the vinegar and Worcestershire sauce and reduce for another 5 minutes or until thickened slightly. Strain into a bowl.

Preheat your barbecue grill plate to high. Generously brush the ribs with the reduced liquid and grill for 5 minutes on each side or until crispy.

Meanwhile, to make the coleslaw, combine the red and white cabbage, carrot and onion in a large bowl. Whisk together the horseradish cream, aioli, lemon juice, oil and mustard, then add to the cabbage mixture. Season with salt and pepper and toss together well.

Serve the ribs fresh from the barbie with the coleslaw.

# CRUMBED PORK CUTLETS
## WITH MINTED POTATO SALAD

This dish is a Spanish classic. It is very hard to overcook or get wrong as once the crumb is cooked to perfection you can just finish it in the oven, where the crumb coating preserves the juiciness of the chop. I like to crumb it all the way down over the bone so I can scrape off all that lovely flavour at the end.

The potato salad here is one of my absolute favourites. Bring it to a picnic or barbecue and everybody will love you. It goes really well with roast chook, too.

There are few special things in this photo. The bull sits on my table at home and represents Spanish strength – it's our national totem. My house is full of them. The knife pictured here is the last thing my best friend, Estephane, gave me before he passed away. It is a beautiful memento and I'm so glad we got it into this shot.

3 teaspoons Cajun spice
4–6 pork cutlets
3 tablespoons plain flour
2 eggs
60 g (1 cup) panko breadcrumbs
1 tablespoon thyme leaves
olive oil, for shallow-frying
salt flakes
lemon wedges, to serve

### MINTED POTATO SALAD
700 g desiree potatoes, peeled and cut into 4 cm cubes
4 spring onions, trimmed and finely sliced
1 bunch of mint, leaves picked and finely sliced
finely grated zest and juice of 2 lemons
2 tablespoons extra-virgin olive oil
200 g thickly sliced ham, cut into cubes
250 g (1 cup) My Quick Aioli (see page 29) or mayonnaise
salt flakes and freshly ground black pepper

**SERVES 4**

Preheat the oven to 170°C (fan-forced).

To make the potato salad, place the potato in a saucepan of cold salted water and bring to the boil. Cook for 10–12 minutes until tender, then drain well.

Meanwhile, combine the spring onion, mint and lemon zest in a large bowl.

Heat 1 tablespoon of the oil in a frying pan over high heat. Add the ham and cook for 2–3 minutes until crisp and caramelised. Add to the bowl with the spring onion mixture. Add the potato while it's still hot and gently toss to combine. Set aside for 5 minutes to cool, then add the aioli or mayo and lemon juice. Season well with salt and pepper and toss to coat and combine. Set aside.

Sprinkle the Cajun spice on both sides of the pork cutlets and rub into the flesh until evenly coated. Place the flour in a shallow bowl, beat the eggs in another bowl, and tip the breadcrumbs and thyme into a third bowl. Coat each cutlet in flour, shaking off the excess, then dip in the egg and finally coat in the breadcrumbs.

Pour oil into a large frying pan to a depth of about 5 mm and heat over medium–high heat. Add the cutlets and cook for 2–3 minutes on each side until golden and just cooked through (the timing will depend on the thickness of the cutlets). Remove and drain on paper towel for 1 minute, seasoning with a pinch of salt, then transfer to the pre-heated oven for 5–10 minutes until cooked through.

Divide the pork cutlets among plates and serve with the potato salad and lemon wedges alongside.

# MEATBALL BOLOGNESE

Bolognese lovers alert! Here is something a bit different for you. Spaghetti bolognese is one of the most frequently cooked dishes in Aussie homes, and making it with meatballs like this is a really great alternative.

olive oil, for pan-frying
1 onion, finely chopped
2 garlic cloves, finely sliced
1 carrot, finely chopped
½ leek, 10 cm trimmed off the top,
    well washed and finely chopped
4 thyme sprigs
700 ml tomato passata
500 ml (2 cups) chicken stock
400 g spaghetti
grated parmesan, basil and
    oregano leaves, to serve

## MEATBALLS
200 g chorizo sausage,
    roughly chopped
150 g button mushrooms
½ red onion, finely chopped
4 garlic cloves, crushed
1 tablespoon chopped flat-leaf
    parsley leaves
1 tablespoon chopped chives
2 tablespoons thickened cream
salt flakes and freshly ground
    black pepper
splash of extra-virgin olive oil
1 small red chilli (optional)
500 g beef mince

**SERVES 4**

Preheat the oven to 200°C (fan-forced) and line a baking tray with baking paper.

To make the meatballs, place the chorizo, mushrooms, onion, garlic, parsley, chives, cream, salt, pepper, oil and chilli, if using, in a food processor and blend to a coarse paste. Transfer the paste to a bowl, add the beef mince and mix well with your hands. Roll the mixture into golf ball–sized meatballs, place on the prepared tray and bake for 10–15 minutes until browned.

Heat a good splash of oil in a medium saucepan over medium heat, add the onion, garlic, carrot, leek and thyme and cook for a few minutes until softened. Pour in the passata and stock, bring to a simmer and cook for 5 minutes.

Add the meatballs to the sauce, reduce the heat to low and simmer gently for 5 minutes or until cooked through.

Meanwhile, cook the spaghetti until al dente according to the packet instructions (I recommend cooking it for 40–60 seconds less then the instructions suggest, just to be on the safe side). Drain.

Toss the spaghetti through the meatballs and sauce, garnish with the parmesan and herbs and serve.

# STEAK FRITES
## WITH BLENDER BEARNAISE

I'm always asked for my favourite cut of steak and this is it: the tomahawk. I don't eat steak often, but if I do it's going to be a proper one! This is a great cut for the whole family to share, which is so much better than cooking individual steaks. The edges are great for those who want their steak well done, then further in the middle it's medium–rare and close to the bone rare. The bone preserves all the moisture on the barbecue.

My cheat's bearnaise sauce is so easy – it's just melted butter in a blender with some flavourings! It tastes just like the real thing from a French restaurant, but without all the whisking and the bain marie.

1 large (1.5–1.7 kg) tomahawk
   rib-eye steak, at room temperature
salt flakes and freshly ground
   black pepper
2 tablespoons olive oil
your favourite salad or broccoli
   wedges (see page 44), to serve

### CHIPS
2 kg desiree potatoes
3–4 tablespoons duck fat or olive oil
salt flakes and freshly ground
   black pepper

### BLENDER BEARNAISE
185 ml (¾ cup) dry white wine
125 ml (½ cup) white wine vinegar
1 small golden shallot, finely sliced
pinch of black peppercorns
3 tarragon sprigs, plus 1–2 teaspoons
   chopped leaves
3 sprigs chervil, plus 1–2 teaspoons
   chopped leaves
salt flakes
3 large egg yolks
180 g ghee or clarified butter (see Tip)

### SERVES 4

**TIP**

To make 180 g clarified butter, heat 250 g butter over low heat until the fat and milk solids separate, then strain off the clear butter. Discard the milk solids.

To make the chips, preheat the oven to 200°C (fan-forced). Line two baking trays with baking paper.

Cut the unpeeled potatoes into finger-sized chips. Place in a large saucepan, cover with cold water and bring to the boil over high heat. Reduce the heat to medium and boil for 2 minutes or until almost tender. Drain well. Spread the chips over the prepared trays in a single layer and dry in the oven for 10 minutes. Remove and toss with the duck fat or oil and season with salt and pepper. Spread them out again in a single layer and bake for 20–30 minutes, turning occasionally, until crisp and golden. Season with salt.

Meanwhile, to make the bearnaise, combine the wine, vinegar, shallot, peppercorns, tarragon and chervil sprigs and a pinch of salt in a medium saucepan and boil over high heat for 3 minutes or until reduced by about two-thirds. Strain the liquid through a fine sieve into a small bowl, discarding the solids. Place 3 tablespoons of the vinegar reduction in the beaker of a stick blender, add the egg yolks and a pinch of salt. (Any leftover reduction can be stored in the freezer for another time.)

Melt the ghee or clarified butter in a small saucepan over high heat, then pour into a heatproof jug. Place the stick blender in the base of the beaker and turn it on. With the motor running, slowly pour in the hot ghee until fully emulsified and the sauce is thick and creamy. Season to taste with salt and fold in the chopped tarragon and chervil. Serve immediately, or transfer to a thermos jug and keep warm for up to 1 hour before serving. Bearnaise cannot be cooled and reheated.

Heat a barbecue grill plate until smoking hot. Season the steaks well, then drizzle with the oil and massage it in. Grill, turning once, for 4–6 minutes each side for medium–rare (the internal temperature should read 58°C on a meat thermometer), or until cooked to your liking. Rest in a warm place for 12 minutes.

Carve the steak and serve with the chips and bearnaise sauce, and your choice of salad or greens.

Herb-crusted Roast Beef with Yorkshire
Puddings & Brussels Sprouts, see page 170

# HERB-CRUSTED ROAST BEEF
## WITH YORKSHIRE PUDDINGS & BRUSSELS SPROUTS

Scotch fillet is my favourite cut of beef to roast because it has a bit of fat that goes right through the whole flesh. I prefer Angus to wagyu for roasting, too. Don't be afraid to go for a large cut – that way you will have plenty of leftovers to use for salads and sandwiches throughout the week.

If you're having a roast beef night you have to have Yorkshire puddings and brussels sprouts to make it truly authentic. Very, very hot oil is the secret for the puddings or they won't work. Brussels sprouts had a tough time back in the days of boiling them, but now they are the new trendy veg. They're really nice served like this with almonds and chorizo.

2 kg scotch fillet (I like black Angus)
½ bunch of rosemary, leaves picked
½ bunch of thyme, leaves picked
2 tablespoons salt flakes
3 tablespoons freshly ground
   black pepper
1 tablespoon olive oil

**YORKSHIRE PUDDINGS**
4 eggs
150 ml milk
250 g (1⅔ cups) plain flour
salt flakes
150 ml chilled water
240 ml sunflower or vegetable oil

**BRUSSELS SPROUTS WITH
CHORIZO AND ALMONDS**
2 chorizo sausages, diced
1 tablespoon olive oil
600 g brussels sprouts, trimmed
   and quartered
60 g unsalted butter
juice of 1 lemon
80 g flaked almonds, toasted
½ bunch of chives, finely sliced
salt flakes and freshly ground
   black pepper

**GRAVY**
3 tablespoons plain flour
250 ml (1 cup) beef stock
40 g butter
salt flakes and freshly ground
   black pepper

**SERVES 10**

Preheat the oven to 240°C (fan-forced). Remove the beef from the fridge and truss with kitchen twine at 5 cm intervals. Allow to come to room temperature.

Place the rosemary, thyme, salt and pepper on a board and finely chop together. Roll the beef in the herb mix to coat evenly.

Heat the olive oil in a deep heatproof roasting tin over medium heat and seal the meat on all sides until golden brown. This locks in the juices and starts to form a crust.

Reduce the oven temperature to 170°C (fan-forced). Transfer the tin to the oven and roast the beef for 1¼ hours for medium–rare or until cooked to your liking. Transfer the beef to a board, cover with foil and leave it to rest while you cook the puddings and make the gravy. Reserve the pan juices for the gravy.

While the beef is cooking, prepare the batter for the Yorkshire puddings. Crack the eggs into a bowl, add the milk and beat together until smooth. Sift the flour into a large bowl and add a generous pinch of salt. Make a well in the centre, then add the egg mixture and whisk to form a smooth batter. Mix in the cold water, then leave the batter to rest at room temperature for 15 minutes.

Once the beef is out of the oven, crank up the temperature as high as it will go. Add 1 tablespoon of oil to each hole of a standard 12-hole muffin tin and place in the oven for 10 minutes to heat up. They must be super hot! Carefully remove the tin from the oven, then pour the rested batter evenly into the holes.

Immediately put the tin back in the oven and cook for 15–20 minutes until the puddings are puffed up and browned. Keep an eye on them towards the end of the cooking time, but don't open the oven until they're beautifully golden, otherwise they will collapse. They should come out just as you are dishing up.

While the puddings are baking, get on with the sprouts. I find it best to cook them in two batches to ensure plenty of caramelisation. Heat a large frying pan over high heat, add half the chorizo and cook for 3–4 minutes until crisp and the red oil is released. Add 2 teaspoons of oil and half the sprouts and toss to combine, then cook for another 5 minutes until the sprouts are tender and beginning to caramelise. Tip onto a plate and wipe the pan clean. Repeat with the remaining chorizo, oil and sprouts. Return the cooked sprouts to the pan, add the butter and lemon juice and toss through. Remove from the heat and sprinkle with toasted almonds and chives. Season to taste.

For the gravy, heat a large frying pan over high heat. Add the strained juices from the roasting tin and bring to a simmer. Whisk in the flour until thickened and smooth. Gradually add the beef stock, whisking to combine, then whisk in the butter. Season with salt and pepper.

Carve the roast beef across the grain and serve with the chorizo sprouts, Yorkshire puddings and gravy.

*Pictured on pages 168–169.*

# BARBECUED HARISSA LAMB
## WITH BABA & MEDITERRANEAN BEAN SALAD

This is a great way to use a nice shoulder or leg of lamb. Harissa paste is available in tubes at the supermarket and it's such a simple way to add flavour to your dishes. Use your hands to really massage it into the lamb – the warmth of your hands will help bring the meat to room temperature ready for cooking. You don't want to burn the beautiful red harissa, so remember to keep turning the lamb. For the baba, it is best to cook the eggplant on an open flame. Don't be afraid to push it so far that it's almost falling apart – the more you burn the outside, the more it steams and softens on the inside. Make sure to slice the lamb against the grain to preserve its tenderness.

1–1.5 kg deboned, butterflied leg
   of lamb
70 g harissa paste
generous pinch of salt flakes
olive oil, for pan-frying

**BABA GHANOUSH**
2 large eggplants
2 garlic cloves, crushed
1 tablespoon tahini
juice of 1 lemon
salt flakes
1½ tablespoons extra-virgin olive oil
1 bunch of chives, chopped

**MEDITERRANEAN BEAN SALAD**
400 g canned butter beans,
   drained and rinsed
1 red chilli, deseeded and
   finely diced
1 golden shallot, finely diced
½ bunch of chives, finely chopped
½ bunch of coriander, leaves picked
½ bunch of mint, leaves picked
2 tablespoons roughly chopped
   Sicilian or Manzanilla olives
3 tablespoons whole-egg
   mayonnaise
salt flakes and freshly ground
   black pepper

**SERVES 6**

Pat the lamb dry with paper towel, then rub all over with the harissa paste and season generously with salt. Keep it out of the fridge for at least 30 minutes prior to cooking so it comes to room temperature. Massaging the meat will also help with this.

Heat a barbecue grill to medium and add a splash of oil. Add the lamb and cook, turning regularly, for 35–40 minutes for medium–rare, or until cooked to your liking. Keep the heat at medium so you don't burn the harissa.

While the lamb is cooking, make the baba and salad so everything is ready at the same time.

For the baba ghanoush, place the eggplants on an open flame for about 10 minutes until charred and blackened all over and the flesh is soft. Place on a chopping board to cool slightly, then peel off the burnt skin, being very careful of the steam. Discard the skin and stems and place the flesh in a bowl. Add the remaining ingredients and mash with a fork until roughly combined, but still retaining some texture.

To make the bean salad, gently toss together all the ingredients in a bowl. Taste and adjust the seasoning if needed.

Finely slice the lamb against the grain and serve on top of the salad, with the baba ghanoush on the side.

# LAMB MONTADITOS
## WITH CHUNKY ROMESCO SAUCE

Montaditos are little sandwiches. I use lamb backstrap when making these, as it's a very easy cut to carve for sandwiches and its long shape means there is plenty of surface area for caramelisation. Romesco sauce is Spain's answer to ketchup – it goes with everything and really makes these sandwiches.

1 baguette, cut into 16 slices
extra-virgin olive oil, for drizzling
salt flakes
200 g soft Persian feta
baby rocket leaves, to serve

**CHUNKY ROMESCO SAUCE**
2 large red capsicums
1–2 long red chillies, or to taste
60 g (½ cup) slivered almonds,
    toasted and roughly chopped
1 garlic clove, finely chopped
3 tablespoons grated fresh tomato
2 tablespoons chopped flat-leaf
    parsley leaves
2 tablespoons red wine vinegar
1 teaspoon smoked paprika
½ teaspoon cayenne pepper
    (optional)
125 ml (½ cup) extra-virgin olive oil
salt flakes and freshly ground
    black pepper

**LAMB**
4 lamb backstraps
1 tablespoon chopped rosemary
    leaves
2 garlic cloves, finely chopped
3 tablespoons olive oil
1 teaspoon salt flakes

**SERVES 8**

To make the romesco sauce, grill the whole capsicums and chillies on hot coals or a barbecue grill, turning regularly, until the skin is black and blistered. Transfer to a board and scrape off the skin. Discard the skin, seeds and membranes and roughly chop the flesh. Place in a bowl, add the remaining ingredients and mix well. Taste and adjust the seasoning if needed.

To prepare the lamb, place the lamb, rosemary, garlic, oil and salt in a bowl and mix well to coat.

Grill over coals or on a barbecue grill, turning once, for 4–6 minutes or until cooked to your liking. Remove and rest for 6 minutes, then finely slice.

While grilling the lamb, working in batches if necessary, grill the bread slices over coals or on the barbecue grill until crisp and golden. Drizzle over a little oil and season lightly with salt.

Spread a slice of baguette with Persian feta, then two slices of lamb, a dollop of romesco, a small handful of rocket and top with another slice of baguette. Repeat with the remaining ingredients to make eight little sandwiches in total.

# PIZZA & BREAD

# WORLD CHAMPION PIZZAS

*I learned how to make pizzas from a world champion: Johnny Di Francesco of 400 Gradi in Melbourne. The secret is to keep it really simple when it comes to toppings. You'll be amazed by the difference that proving the dough makes, too. Sourdough pizzas like this have yeast in the dough; the more you prove it the more it ferments and the more digestible it becomes. This way, you can eat plenty of pizza without feeling full!*

*I have given some simple topping ideas below. You can even try stuffing cheese sticks into the crust for the kids! I don't recommend freezing leftover dough – roll any excess into little balls, stuff them with cheese and pop them in the oven to make mini bread rolls.*

500 g fresh mozzarella or
　fior di latte, torn
extra-virgin olive oil, for drizzling
salt flakes and freshly ground
　black pepper

## PIZZA DOUGH

1½ tablespoons fine sea salt
1 kg '00' flour, plus extra
　for dusting
3 g fresh yeast

## TOMATO SAUCE

3–4 tablespoons extra-virgin
　olive oil, plus extra for drizzling
2 garlic cloves, finely sliced
2 kg ripe roma or oxheart
　tomatoes, grated
½ bunch of basil, leaves picked
salt flakes and freshly ground
　black pepper

## MAKES 8

## FAVOURITE TOPPINGS

- Pepperoni and chorizo,
　finely sliced
- Pesto on the base (instead of
　tomato) with feta and black olives
- Fold cheese sticks into the crust, use
　garlic oil instead of the sauce and
　finish with oregano and za'atar
- Four cheeses: vintage cheddar,
　triple cream brie, parmesan and
　truffle manchego
- Folded calzone style, with
　meatballs and cheeses

To make the dough, place the salt in a large bowl, add 600 ml of lukewarm water and stir to dissolve. Add 75 g (½ cup) of the flour and mix well, then add a little more flour and the yeast and mix again. Gradually add the remaining flour and mix to form a dough. Turn out onto a lightly floured surface and knead for 10 minutes or until smooth and elastic. Place the dough in a lightly floured bowl, cover with a damp cloth and rest in a warm place for just over an hour or until doubled in size.

Meanwhile, for the sauce, heat the oil in a large wide-based saucepan over medium heat, add the garlic and cook gently for 1 minute. Add the tomato, half the basil leaves and a pinch of salt and pepper. Reduce the heat to low and simmer for 35–45 minutes until very thick. Season to taste, then leave to cool completely.

Place the rested dough on a lightly floured bench. Lightly knead, then divide evenly into eight balls and rest, uncovered, for 40 minutes.

Preheat the oven to 180°C (fan-forced).

If you're using a pizza stone on the barbecue, make sure the stone is really hot before you put the pizza on it. If you're cooking on the barbecue with no pizza stone, put it on the hot plate for the first minute until the base is seared, then move it to the grill (which is off) and close the hood for 90 seconds. The residual heat from the hot plate will be enough here.

If you're cooking in a pizza oven at 300°C it should take 90 seconds.

Working with one ball of dough at a time, stretch it out by hand and place on a floured pizza peel or a square of floured baking paper. Use the palm of your hand to press the dough into a large flat disc, then press it out from the centre with your fingers, stretching it into a large circle (though no bigger than a 25 cm dinner plate or pizza tray).

Spread a thin layer of tomato sauce over the base, leaving a 1 cm border for crust formation. Top with torn mozzarella or fior di latte and scatter with a few of the remaining basil leaves. Drizzle with oil and season to taste with salt and pepper.

Bake in batches for 5–8 minutes until the edges are blistered, golden and crispy.

Barbecued Yoghurt Flatbreads (Coca Catalana), see page 182
Beetroot Flatbreads with Koftas & Minty Yoghurt, see page 183

# BARBECUED YOGHURT FLATBREADS
## (COCA CATALANA)

This is the simplest recipe in the universe. Using a food processor means there's no kneading involved, and you don't have to prove the dough either. You can be really inventive when it comes to mixing different herbs and spices through the dough – as long as you keep the basic ratios the same, it'll work. You can also cut the flatbreads into little wedges to use on a cheese board. Whatever you do, always grill the bread and then eat it straight away. So rewarding.

500 g (3 ⅓ cups) self-raising flour, plus extra if needed and for dusting
500 g (2 cups) Greek yoghurt, plus extra if needed
6 thyme sprigs, leaves picked
4 rosemary sprigs, leaves picked
splash of extra-virgin olive oil, plus extra for brushing
salt flakes and freshly ground black pepper

**SERVES 6**

Preheat a barbecue hot plate to medium.

Place the flour in a large bowl and make a well in the centre. Add the yoghurt, thyme, rosemary and oil and season with salt and pepper. Mix with your hands until the dough comes together. If the dough is too dry, add more yoghurt; if it's too wet, add more flour.

Turn out the dough onto a floured surface and knead gently to bring it into a smooth ball. Divide into six even portions.

Use a rolling pin to roll each piece into a long oval shape, about 5 mm thick. Brush with olive oil and grill on the barbecue for about 4 minutes on each side until cooked through with attractive grill marks.

To finish, preheat the oven to 180°C (fan-forced).

Choose some toppings from the list below and flash in the oven for 2 minutes.

*Pictured on pages 180–181.*

### FAVOURITE TOPPINGS

- Barbecued field mushrooms, finely sliced, with grilled haloumi
- Roasted vegetables, such as pumpkin and baby beetroot, with labne
- 'Nduja, manchego and green olives
- Sliced piquillos and anchovies
- Garlic prawns and steamed pippies
- Artichoke hearts and good-quality tuna or bacalao
- Grilled lamb and salsa verde

# BEETROOT FLATBREADS
## WITH KOFTAS & MINTY YOGHURT

*This is a great spin on the basic flatbread recipe opposite. Beetroot is one of my favourite vegetables so I like to use it as much as possible, but you can use whatever veggies or flavourings you like.*

1 small beetroot, peeled and diced
80 g (⅓ cup) Greek yoghurt
150–225 g (1–1½ cups) self-raising
  flour, plus extra for dusting
olive oil spray
mint leaves, to serve

**MINTY YOGHURT DRESSING**
250 g (1 cup) Greek yoghurt
1 bunch of mint, leaves picked
  and finely chopped
½ teaspoon ground cumin
1 small garlic clove, crushed
1 tablespoon honey
pinch of salt flakes
extra-virgin olive oil, for drizzling

**KOFTAS**
500 g beef mince
1 small onion, grated
2 garlic cloves, crushed
1 teaspoon ground coriander
1 teaspoon ground cumin
1 teaspoon ground cinnamon
3 tablespoons dried breadcrumbs
1 egg
2 teaspoons salt flakes
½ teaspoon freshly ground
  black pepper
2 tablespoons extra-virgin olive oil

**SERVES 4**

Place the beetroot and yoghurt in a blender and blitz until smooth. Transfer to a medium bowl, add 150 g (1 cup) of the flour and bring together with a spatula until just combined, then use your hands to form into a ball. Add a little more flour if it's too sticky or wet.

Heat a chargrill pan or barbecue grill plate over medium–high heat.

Pinch off a golf ball–sized piece of dough and roll it into a ball on a well-floured bench. Flatten with the palm of your hand and dust with flour, then turn the flatbread over and press again into a 10 cm round. Spray with olive oil, then grill for 1 minute or until grill marks appear on the base and bubbles begin to form on the top. Spray with oil, then flip over and cook for another minute. Remove and repeat with the remaining dough to make eight flatbreads in total.

To make the minty yoghurt dressing, stir the ingredients together in a serving bowl and place in the fridge until you are ready to serve. Just before serving, drizzle with olive oil. Alternatively, place all the ingredients in a blender and blend until bright green and well combined.

For the koftas, place all the ingredients, except the oil, in a large bowl and mix until well combined. Divide into eight to ten even portions. With damp hands, roll each portion into a log shape, then thread onto metal skewers.

Heat 1 tablespoon of oil in a large frying pan over medium heat. Add two or three koftas and cook, turning to brown evenly, for 5 minutes or until cooked through. Remove and drain on paper towel. Repeat with the remaining oil and koftas.

Serve the flatbreads with the koftas, a dollop of yoghurt sauce and sprinkle of mint leaves.

*Pictured on pages 180–181.*

# VEGGIE-PACKED GOZLEME

Gozleme are delicious stuffed Turkish flatbreads and a popular street food around the world. If I ever see a gozleme stall I'll order one, even if I'm not really hungry! My version uses a very easy and forgiving dough, with paprika and lots of olive oil. It will always work, even if it is slightly over- or undercooked. You can make the gozleme any size you like and really play around with the fillings. I like to grate the veggies finely so they almost disappear into the cheese (a great way to hide them from your kids). Always finish with just a squeeze of lemon. No sauce required!

½ head of cauliflower, grated
½ head of broccoli, grated
1 carrot, grated
1 beetroot, grated
200 g soft Persian feta
100 g baby spinach leaves
extra-virgin olive oil, for brushing
lemon wedges, to serve

**DOUGH**

1 x 7 g sachet instant dried yeast
1 teaspoon caster sugar
1 teaspoon salt flakes
450 g (3 cups) plain flour
1 tablespoon smoked paprika
80 ml (⅓ cup) extra-virgin
    olive oil

**SERVES 4**

To make the dough, combine the yeast, sugar, salt and 90 ml of lukewarm water in a small bowl and set aside for 10 minutes until it begins to bubble and activate. Mix together the flour and paprika in a large bowl and make a well in the centre. Add the yeast mixture, oil and 200 ml of lukewarm water. Working from the centre, slowly mix to incorporate the flour, stirring until a rough dough starts to form. Turn out onto a lightly floured surface and knead for 10 minutes until smooth and elastic. Place the dough in a lightly oiled bowl and set aside, covered, for 45 minutes or until doubled in size.

Meanwhile, heat a barbecue hot plate or large frying pan over medium heat.

Turn out the dough onto a lightly floured surface and lightly knead, then divide into four even pieces. Roll each piece into a rectangle about 30 cm x 20 cm. Sprinkle the grated vegetables evenly over two of the rectangles, leaving a little space around the edges, then crumble over the feta and finish with the spinach leaves. Top with the two remaining rectangles of dough and pinch the edges together to seal, keeping the join as thin as possible.

Lightly brush each gozleme with oil and cook on the hot plate or frying pan for 3–4 minutes on each side or until golden. Remove from the heat, cut into quarters and serve with lemon wedges.

DESSERTS

# TARTA DE SANTIAGO

Tarta de Santiago (cake of Saint James) comes from the beautiful Spanish city of Galicia. Traditionally, it is sold along the route of the famous Camino de Santiago pilgrimage trail – a delicious burst of energy for the faithful. To qualify as authentic, it needs to be at least thirty-three per cent almonds and made in Galicia ... well, I guess this can be our Australian version!

I make mine a bit special by putting chocolate chips through the almond filling as a little surprise. For a truly Insta-worthy dessert, make sure you google the Santiago cross, then print and cut one out to make a stencil. Once the cake has cooled slightly, place the stencil on top and dust with icing sugar to get this stunning look.

250 g (1 ⅔ cups) plain flour
75 g icing sugar, plus extra
  for dusting
125 g chilled unsalted butter,
  chopped
3 egg yolks
pinch of salt flakes
double cream, to serve

**FILLING**
125 g unsalted butter, softened
50 g caster sugar
2 eggs
100 g (1 cup) almond meal
1 teaspoon plain flour
finely grated zest of 1 orange
finely grated zest of 1 lemon
75 g dark chocolate chips

**SERVES 6-8**

Sift the flour and icing sugar into the bowl of a food processor, add the butter and process until crumbly. Add the egg yolks and salt and blend until combined. Tip out the dough and press together into a ball, then wrap in plastic wrap and rest in the fridge for 1 hour.

Preheat the oven to 175°C (fan-forced). Grease a 24 cm round loose-based flan tin.

Roll out the dough between two sheets of baking paper until large enough to line the base and side of the prepared tin. Lift the dough into the tin and gently press into the edges. Refrigerate for 15 minutes.

Line the pastry with baking paper and fill with uncooked rice or baking beans. Blind-bake for 10 minutes, then remove the paper and weights. Return to the oven for another 5 minutes or until the tart shell is dry and lightly golden. Set aside to cool completely.

Meanwhile, to make the filling, place the butter and sugar in the small bowl of a stand mixer fitted with the paddle attachment and beat until light and creamy. Add the eggs one at a time, beating between additions, then stir in the almond meal, flour, zest and chocolate chips. Spoon the filling into the tart shell and smooth the top.

Bake for 30–35 minutes until the tip of a knife or a skewer inserted in the centre comes out clean. Allow to cool completely, then release from the tin. Dust generously with extra icing sugar and serve with double cream.

## LEMON, THYME & VANILLA
# APPLE CRUMBLE

This winter warmer is super easy to make and a great dessert to share. Pink ladies are my favourite apples, but feel free to use any that are in season. The secret to this dish is using top-quality vanilla and fresh, sweet thyme. When making the crumble topping, be mindful that less mixing is more – use your fingers so your body temperature melts the butter quickly and make sure to keep the mixture nice and coarse. Serve the crumble piping hot so the ice cream melts into it … with all that fruit you won't feel too guilty.

50 g unsalted butter
6 thyme sprigs, leaves picked
1 vanilla bean, split and seeds scraped
1.25 kg pink lady apples, peeled, cored and cut into wedges
1½ teaspoons ground cinnamon
½ nutmeg, freshly grated
2 tablespoons caster sugar
finely grated zest of 2 lemons
vanilla ice cream, to serve (optional)

### CRUMBLE
110 g (¾ cup) plain flour
110 g almond meal
110 g caster sugar
110 g chilled unsalted butter, chopped

**SERVES 6**

Melt the butter in a large frying pan over medium heat. Add the thyme and vanilla bean and seeds and cook, stirring, for 2 minutes to infuse the butter. Increase the heat to high, add the apple and cook, tossing regularly, for 5 minutes. Stir in the cinnamon and nutmeg and cook for 1–2 minutes until aromatic. Add 3 tablespoons of water, then reduce the heat to medium and cook, stirring regularly, for another 5–6 minutes until the apple starts to soften. Take off the heat and remove the vanilla bean.

Lightly grease a 28 cm x 18 cm baking dish with butter. Spoon in the apple mixture and scatter over the sugar and lemon zest. Set aside to cool for 20 minutes.

Preheat the oven to 190°C (fan-forced).

To make the crumble, place all the ingredients in a bowl. Using your fingertips, rub the butter into the dry ingredients until the mixture resembles very coarse breadcrumbs.

Spread the crumble evenly over the apple mixture, then place in the oven and bake for 20–25 minutes until golden.

Serve warm with ice cream, if you like.

# BANOFFEE PIE

There is something very special about the marriage of banana and toffee, and the honeymoon baby is the famous banoffee pie. It's a real favourite of mine. If you don't want to make your own caramel (dulce de leche) like we've done here, you can buy it pre-made. Try getting a bit fancy by using a blowtorch to caramelise the banana and a peeler, mandoline or microplane to shave chocolate over the top. Make sure your bananas are nice and ripe for a more intense flavour.

200 g can sweetened
   condensed milk
155 ml milk
7 small ripe bananas
100 g caster sugar
80 g (½ cup) unsalted macadamia
   nuts, toasted and crushed
1 ready-made pie crust or tart base
   (or use the tart base from the
   Tarta de Santiago, see page 191)
250 ml double cream
1 x 100 g block dark chocolate
   (optional)
1 x 100 g block white chocolate
   (optional)

**SERVES 6–8**

Place the unopened can of condensed milk in a large saucepan of water, making sure it is completely submerged, and boil for 4 hours. Check it often and top up the water as required. If the pan boils dry the can will likely explode, sending caramel into every nook and cranny of your kitchen! Remove and cool completely before you open the can.

Using a stick blender, combine the milk with three of the bananas.

Pour the sugar into a medium saucepan over high heat and let it melt, without stirring, until it forms a dark caramel. Add the blended banana and whisk until combined. Stir in the crushed macadamias.

Pour the mixture into the pastry case and place in the fridge to set for at least 30 minutes.

Whip the cream to soft peaks, then gently fold in the condensed milk caramel.

Peel and slice the remaining bananas. Arrange the slices over the pie filling, then dollop the caramel cream on top.

Shave dark and/or white chocolate on top, if you like, and serve.

*Churros con Chocolate, see page 198*
*Orange Flans, see page 199*

# CHURROS CON CHOCOLATE

This my most frequently requested recipe! It's one I'm very proud of and something I've been making for years. In Spain, there are two different types of churros: the really thin and crispy ones and the big, thick variety known as porras. My version combines the two, so you have the super crispy outside and the almost undercooked, creamy centre. Perfection. I used to make 300 of these to order per day at my restaurant.

For perfect churros, you need to make the batter and then fry it straight away – fresh is best. After frying, quickly drain the churros on paper towel, then plunge them straight into the sugar while still hot to get that lovely crust. This is a non-non-sugar-free recipe! If you like, you can thicken up the chocolate sauce with condensed milk or add a splash of olive oil to make it glossier (this is a good trick if you're not using the best-quality chocolate). You can add a splash of alcohol to the sauce, too. You'll need a number 9 or 10 star piping nozzle (2 cm wide) for this recipe.

250 ml (1 cup) milk
1 teaspoon caster sugar,
  plus extra for dusting
50 g unsalted butter, chopped
1 vanilla bean, split and seeds
  scraped
120 g plain flour
2 egg yolks
vegetable oil, for deep-frying

**CHOCOLATE SAUCE**
200 g dark chocolate, chopped
150 ml milk
2 tablespoons sweetened
  condensed milk, or to taste

**SERVES 4**

To make the chocolate sauce, place the chocolate in a heatproof bowl. Bring the milk to the boil in a small saucepan, then pour over the chocolate and whisk until melted and smooth. Gradually add the condensed milk until the sauce is your preferred consistency – the more you add, the thicker (and sweeter) it will be.

Combine the milk, sugar, butter and vanilla bean and seeds in a medium saucepan and bring to the boil. Remove the vanilla bean and reduce the heat to low. Sift in the flour and whisk until combined and the dough comes away from the side of the pan. Remove from the heat and set aside to cool for 3 minutes. Beat in the egg yolks, one at a time.

Spoon the dough into a piping bag fitted with a 2 cm star nozzle.

Pour the oil for deep-frying into a large heavy-based saucepan and heat over high heat to 180°C. Working in batches so you don't overcrowd the pan, pipe 7 cm lengths of dough into the oil, cutting it off with a sharp knife. Deep-fry the churros for 3–4 minutes or until golden brown, then remove with a slotted spoon and drain on paper towel.

Dust with extra caster sugar while still hot and serve with the chocolate sauce.

*Pictured on page 196.*

**TIP**

If you don't want your chocolate sauce to be too sweet, you can omit the condensed milk and add a dash of Frangelico, Kahlua, rum, sherry or Baileys instead.

# ORANGE FLANS

Growing up, this was the dessert my mum would make all the time. It's very authentic. A bit like a Spanish version of creme brulee, it's a set custard with an insane orange flavour. I recommend making these really small, using wide, shallow ceramic dishes rather than dariole moulds or muffin trays. A thinner surface allows for more caramelisation and they'll steam and set very fast.

You can omit the Cointreau in the caramel if you like, but most of the alcohol will burn off anyway so they'll still be fine to share with the family.

625 ml (2 ½ cups) milk
2 vanilla beans, split and
    seeds scraped
finely grated zest of 2 oranges
3 eggs
2 egg yolks
160 g pure icing sugar, sifted

CARAMEL
220 g caster sugar
1 tablespoon Cointreau
2 teaspoons orange juice

SERVES 6

Preheat the oven to 170°C (fan-forced). Place six 13 cm x 3 cm deep round ovenproof dishes in a deep roasting tin.

To make the caramel, combine the sugar and 250 ml (1 cup) of water in a medium heavy-based saucepan over medium heat and stir, without boiling, until the sugar has dissolved. Use a wet pastry brush to brush any stray grains of sugar on the side back into the mixture. Bring to the boil and cook, without stirring, until the caramel begins to turn a light golden brown. Add the Cointreau and juice and stir until combined.

Pour 5 mm of caramel into each ovenproof dish and leave to set at room temperature. Don't put it in the fridge or the caramel will separate.

Place the milk, vanilla beans and seeds and orange zest in a medium saucepan over low heat and gently bring to the boil. Take off the heat and stand 5 minutes. Remove the vanilla beans.

Lightly whisk the eggs, egg yolks and icing sugar in a medium bowl. Gradually add the infused milk and whisk to combine.

Pour the custard evenly into the dishes, then pour boiling water into the roasting tin to come halfway up the side of the dishes. Bake for 30 minutes or until the custards are just set, with a slight wobble. Remove and cool to room temperature, then place in the fridge overnight.

Run a knife around the edges to loosen the custards, then invert onto plates, allowing the caramel sauce to coat the flans.

*Pictured on page 197.*

# SHOW-STOPPING STRAWBERRY CHEESECAKE

I feel like I've been to every single strawberry farm in Australia with my TV gigs. It's turned me into a bit of a strawberry aficionado – there are so many different types and varieties to suit different purposes. But you know what? The ones in the supermarket are great. The trick to this dish is to choose strawberries that are all the same size so your finished dish looks spot on. Keep the greens on for presentation, then just remove them as you eat. It's important to use a good-quality marmalade or jam for this cheesecake – have a look at your local farmers' market as good jam really makes a difference.

75 g strawberry jam
juice of ½ lemon
500 g strawberries, halved,
   with green tops on one half
   of each strawberry

**BISCUIT BASE**
300 g shortbread biscuits
75 g unsalted butter, softened
2 lavender sprigs, flowers picked,
   or ¼ teaspoon dried lavender
   flowers (optional)

**FILLING**
750 g cream cheese, at room
   temperature
90 g (¾ cup) pure icing sugar
1 vanilla bean, split and
   seeds scraped
finely grated zest of 1 lemon
300 ml double cream

**SERVES 6-8**

Grease a 23 cm springform tin with butter.

To make the biscuit base, place the shortbread, butter and lavender, if using, in a food processor and pulse to a coarse crumb. Press the mixture into the base of the tin, using the base of a jar or glass to flatten it out evenly.

Mix together the jam and lemon juice until smooth. Spread over the biscuit base and refrigerate for 10 minutes.

Meanwhile, to make the filling, beat the cream cheese, icing sugar, vanilla seeds and lemon zest until smooth. Gradually add the double cream, whisking until combined.

Remove the tin from the fridge and spread the filling over the jam layer, smoothing the top with a spatula. Place in the fridge to set for at least 1 hour or overnight. Before decorating the top, put the cheesecake in the freezer for 30 minutes.

Smooth any rough edges with a spatula, then press the strawberries, cut-side up, into the top, forming a circle fanning out from the centre. Decorate half with the strawberries with green tops, and the other side with those without. Serve immediately.

# STICKY DATE PUDDING

There is something very special about this classic, warming comfort food. You need the perfect size dish to get the proportions right – too large and the pudding will be too thin, too small and it will be undercooked in the middle. Be adventurous with your butterscotch sauce – try a spicy schnapps or whisky, or even a pinch of salt for a salted caramel flavour – and make sure you DRENCH the pudding with sauce.

240 g medjool dates, pitted
1 teaspoon bicarbonate of soda
200 ml boiling water
90 g unsalted butter, softened
160 g caster sugar
2 large eggs
165 g self-raising flour
pinch of ground cinnamon
¼ nutmeg, freshly grated
1 tablespoon malt powder
2 tablespoons creme fraiche
1 tablespoon double cream
vanilla ice cream, to serve

## BUTTERSCOTCH SAUCE
50 g unsalted butter
180 g brown sugar
150 ml double cream
1 vanilla bean, split and
  seeds scraped
2 teaspoons butterscotch
  schnapps (optional)

**SERVES 8**

Preheat the oven to 175°C (fan-forced). Grease and line a 21 cm x 11 cm loaf tin with baking paper.

Place the dates in a heatproof bowl, add the bicarbonate of soda and boiling water and set aside for 5 minutes until softened. Blend to a chunky puree in a food processor.

Meanwhile, beat the butter and caster sugar until pale. Add the eggs, flour, cinnamon, nutmeg and malt and mix well. Using a spatula, fold in the creme fraiche, double cream and pureed dates.

Pour the batter into the prepared tin and bake for 40 minutes.

To make the sauce, melt the butter in a wide saucepan over medium heat, add the brown sugar and 70 ml of the cream and whisk until smooth. Simmer without stirring for 2 minutes, then add the vanilla seeds and remove from the heat. Stir in the remaining cream and the schnapps, if using. Leave to cool slightly.

Serve the warm sticky date pudding with lots of butterscotch sauce and some vanilla ice cream on the side.

# BASQUE BURNT CHEESECAKE

This delicious Spanish classic has become a real favourite in Australia over the last few years – everyone wants to know how to make it! Well, it is a very simple recipe. The secret? Make sure you burn it. This is the only time you're allowed to burn your food in the kitchen, haha! But seriously, there is a very fine line between caramelised and burnt – finding that edge is the secret to this dish. Keep a close eye on it during the last 15 minutes of cooking. This cheesecake is best served at room temperature.

585 g cream cheese, at room
    temperature
4 eggs, at room temperature
245 g caster sugar
290 ml thickened cream
    (minimum 35% fat)
3 tablespoons cornflour
pinch of salt flakes

**SERVES 6-8**

Preheat the oven to 200°C (fan-forced). Grease a 23 cm springform tin and line with crushed baking paper, extending it 2 cm over the edge.

Beat the cream cheese until smooth and creamy. Add the eggs, one at a time, beating well after each addition. Gradually beat in the sugar, then the cream. Add the cornflour and salt and beat until smooth.

Pour the batter into the prepared tin and tap gently on the bench to remove any air bubbles. Rest for 5 minutes, then bake for 55 minutes or until the top is dark brown and a skewer inserted in the centre comes out clean. Switch off the oven and leave the cheesecake inside to cool to room temperature. (This is important – if you try to remove the cheesecake from the tin while it's still warm it may collapse.)

Remove the cheesecake from the tin and serve. It will keep in an airtight container in the fridge for 1–2 days, but bring it back to room temperature before serving.

# CAKES & BISCUITS

# BANANA JOE LOAF

*Banana Joe* starring Bud Spencer was one of my favourite movies from my childhood. I love the name. I also really love bananas as they're one of the only ingredients that can give you the sweetness of a dessert without using any added sugar. If you really push bananas to the limit of ripeness, when their skin turns completely black, there is no sugar needed in a recipe like this (though a bit of coconut sugar sprinkled on top can be nice for crunch). This is a great lunchbox treat and will keep in fridge covered in plastic wrap for up to one week – just pop slices in the toaster when it starts to gets dry.

250 g (1 ⅔ cups) plain flour
2 tablespoons baking powder
90 g walnuts, roughly chopped
½ teaspoon ground cinnamon
6 overripe bananas (see Tip),
    plus 1 banana extra, sliced in
    half lengthways
125 g unsalted butter, softened
2 eggs, separated
1½ tablespoons maple syrup,
    plus extra for drizzling
coconut sugar, for sprinkling
    (optional)

**SERVES 6–8**

Preheat the oven to 175°C (fan-forced). Grease and flour a 22 cm x 11 cm loaf tin.

Sift the flour and baking powder into a large bowl and stir in the walnuts and cinnamon.

In another bowl, mash the overripe bananas until smooth. Mix through the softened butter, leaving small bits still visible, then add the egg yolks and maple syrup and mix until smooth. Add the flour mixture and stir to combine.

Beat the egg whites until soft peaks form, then gently fold into the banana batter, being sure to keep plenty of air in the mix.

Pour the batter into the prepared tin and smooth the surface. Arrange the extra sliced banana on top. Drizzle with a little extra maple syrup and sprinkle with coconut sugar, if using, then bake for 1 hour or until a skewer inserted in the centre comes out clean. Cool in the tin for a few minutes, then turn out onto a wire rack to cool completely. Cut into thick slices to serve.

**TIP**

Overripe bananas are the key to the best-tasting banana bread as they are sweeter, have more flavour and are easier to mash. And because they have so much natural sweetness, you can use more banana and less sugar! The worse the bananas look, the better they'll be for this recipe.

# MAGGIE'S SHORTBREAD

Maggie is my wife Sascha's mum and my children's granny. She is from Scotland and let me tell you – nobody makes shortbread like a Scot, and especially a Scottish granny. I lived in Scotland for three years so I know this to be true. This recipe was passed down to Maggie from *her* mother, then Maggie passed it down to Sascha, who will in turn give it to our children, Claudia and Morgan. It is an amazing part of our family's cooking legacy. Maggie is the best granny ever, and she will be really proud to see this treasured recipe included here.

125 g (1 cup) icing sugar
250 g unsalted butter, softened
125 g (1 cup) cornflour
250 g (1⅔ cups) plain flour,
    plus extra for dusting
caster sugar, for sprinkling

**SERVES 8**

Preheat the oven to 160°C (fan-forced) and line a large baking tray with baking paper.

Place the icing sugar and butter in a large bowl and beat until smooth.

Sift the flours into a separate bowl, then add to the butter mixture and gently knead to bring the dough together.

Roll out the dough on a lightly floured surface to a rectangle about 3 cm thick. Taking care not to cut all the way through, score the dough into your desired shape, such as squares, and prick with a fork.

Bake for 25 minutes or until lightly golden.

Remove from the oven and finish cutting all the way through the shortbread. Sprinkle with caster sugar while still warm, then set aside to cool. The shortbread will keep in an airtight container for up to 3 days.

# FLOURLESS ALMOND–HAZELNUT
# CHOCOLATE CAKE

I love using nut meals in cakes. They bring a totally different flavour profile and have an amazing, dense texture. The nut meals in this gluten-free cake really enhance the chocolate and orange flavours. This is a great base recipe to make your own with different garnishes – fruit in the middle, whipped cream, ganache or icing on top – but I like mine really simple like this, with nothing but a cup of tea.

This is a great cake to try out with a fancy silicone mould, to get that bundt or doughnut shape. If using a silicone mould, you MUST let the cake cool to room temperature and then pop it in the freezer for an hour before attempting to turn it out. If you invert the cake while still warm, it will break.

150 g dark chocolate
   (70% cocoa solids)
150 ml pouring cream
1 teaspoon finely grated
   orange zest
60 g unsalted butter
55 g pure icing sugar
40 g almond meal
40 g hazelnut meal
½ teaspoon baking powder
4 egg whites
icing sugar, to dust (optional)
extra cream or ice cream,
   to serve (optional)

SERVES 6-8

Preheat the oven to 170°C (fan-forced). Grease a non-stick 22 cm cake tin or silicone mould.

Break the chocolate into pieces and place in a heatproof bowl. Bring the cream to the boil in a small saucepan, then pour over the chocolate, stirring constantly until melted, smooth and shiny. Add the orange zest and leave to cool slightly.

Melt the butter in a small saucepan over low heat just until it develops a slightly nutty aroma – you don't want it to colour too much. Pour into a bowl to stop the cooking process and set aside.

Combine the icing sugar, almond meal, hazelnut meal and baking powder in a bowl.

Lightly beat the egg whites until soft peaks form, then carefully fold into the dry ingredients. Gently stir in the melted butter and then the choc–orange ganache.

Pour the batter into the prepared tin and smooth the surface. Bake for 15 minutes. You want the texture to be quite soft and fudgy so it's much better to undercook this cake than overcook it. Leave to cool completely in the tin, then gently remove and, if you like, dust with icing sugar and serve with cream or ice cream. It's also great as is.

# THE ULTIMATE ICE CREAM CAKE
## WITH HONEYCOMB & A MOLTEN CARAMEL CENTRE

There's nothing better than an ice cream cake in summer. Perfect for birthdays and barbecues, it looks like a million bucks and, better still, you can do all the prep the day before and keep it in the freezer until you're ready to serve.

Made with ready-made ingredients, this cake takes a bit of time between stages and needs to be started a day ahead, but the result is totally worth it. Try to keep the elements evenly spread so that you're hit with three different textures in every slice: the sponge, the crunch of the honeycomb, and the oozy softness of the dulce.

This is my most-liked recipe ever on Instagram, with hundreds and thousands of views. Make sure you post a pic when you make it!

2 x 500 g chocolate swiss roll
  cakes, each cut into 6 thick slices
1 x 370 g packet Oreo biscuits
2 litres vanilla ice cream, softened
cooking oil spray
3 x 150 g Crunchie bars
1 litre chocolate ice cream, softened
1 x 395 g can dulce de leche

### CHOCOLATE SAUCE
500 g dark chocolate
200 ml milk

**SERVES 12**

Line a deep stainless-steel bowl (3 litre capacity) with two layers of plastic wrap. Line the bowl with the cake slices, then cover and freeze for 30 minutes or until firm.

Roughly chop the Oreo biscuits and mix through the vanilla ice cream. Spread over the cake slices in the bowl.

Spray the outside of a smaller (1 litre) bowl with oil and add to the bowl, pressing it against the base and side to create a cavity for the next layer. Cover and freeze for 1 hour.

Roughly chop the Crunchies and mix through the chocolate ice cream. Remove the small bowl from the cake and spoon in the chocolate ice cream mix. Spray the outside of an even smaller bowl (about 400 ml) with oil and add to the bowl, pressing it into the chocolate mixture to make a cavity for the caramel. Cover and freeze for 1 hour.

Remove the small bowl and spoon in the dulce de leche, then cover and freeze overnight.

Just before you are ready to serve, make the chocolate sauce. Break the chocolate into pieces and place in a heatproof bowl. Bring the milk to just below the boil and pour over the chocolate, stirring until smooth and combined.

Remove the bowl from the freezer and invert the cake onto a platter. Lift off the bowl and plastic wrap. Using a hot 30 cm knife, cut the cake into even slices. Serve with the hot chocolate sauce. Leftovers will keep in the freezer for 8 months, but will be eaten long before then!

# DOUBLE CHOC AMERICANO BROWNIES

I learned how to make these in Edinburgh, in the first kitchen I ever worked in – Indigo Yard (very posh). They only had two cakes on the menu: lemon delicious and brownie Americano. I had to prep millions of them before the pastry chef arrived. These brownies have the requisite cracked appearance on top, while the inside has a wonderfully chewy texture from the brown sugar. So what we have here is an American dessert, inspired by a Scottish restaurant, made by a Spanish chef, published in an Australian cookbook!

185 g unsalted butter
375 g dark chocolate (70% cocoa solids), broken into pieces
5 eggs
155 g brown sugar
60 g caster sugar
120 g plain flour, sifted
pinch of salt flakes
100 g milk chocolate, chopped
90 g hazelnuts, lightly toasted and skins removed, roughly chopped

**MAKES 12**

Preheat the oven to 160°C (fan-forced) and line a 30 cm x 20 cm lamington tin with baking paper.

Place the butter and dark chocolate in a heatproof bowl over a saucepan of simmering water (don't let the bowl touch the water). Stir until melted and combined, then remove and set aside to cool.

In a separate bowl, beat the eggs and sugars until light and fluffy. Stir in the cooled chocolate mixture, sifted flour and salt and mix together well. Stir through half the milk chocolate and half the hazelnuts.

Pour the mixture into the prepared tin and smooth the surface. Sprinkle evenly with the remaining chocolate and hazelnuts, then bake for 18 minutes or until a crust forms on top.

Remove from the oven and leave to cool in the tin, then cut into squares and serve. The brownies will keep in an airtight container for up to 5 days.

 **TIPS**

You can use any type of chocolate you like for this recipe – dark, milk or a combination. Anything with more than 50% cocoa solids will work.

For perfect slices, pop the tray in the freezer for 20 minutes, then slice the brownies with a 30 cm knife dipped in hot water.

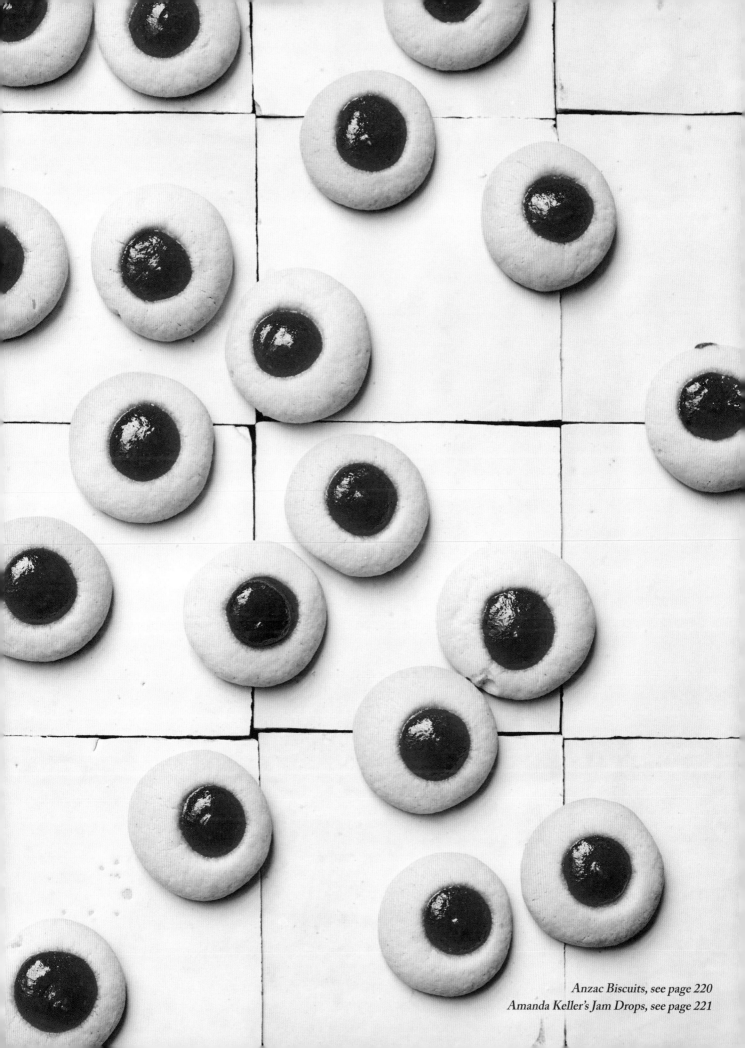

*Anzac Biscuits, see page 220*
*Amanda Keller's Jam Drops, see page 221*

# ANZAC BISCUITS

This is the New Zealand Army's original recipe. With its amazing history, it's no wonder this iconic biscuit is beloved in every New Zealand and Australian home. I have such respect for these troops and their devotion to their service.

125 g unsalted butter
2 tablespoons golden syrup
½ teaspoon bicarbonate of soda
2 tablespoons hot water
200 g caster sugar
80 g (1 cup) desiccated coconut
100 g (⅔ cup) plain flour
100 g (1 cup) rolled oats

**MAKES 20**

Preheat the oven to 170°C (fan-forced). Line two baking trays with baking paper.

Melt the butter in a large saucepan over medium heat, add the golden syrup and stir until combined.

Combine the bicarbonate of soda and water, and stir into the butter mixture. It will foam up briefly.

Remove the pan from the heat and stir in the remaining ingredients.

Take heaped tablespoons of the mixture and roll into evenly sized balls (about 30 g each). Arrange on the prepared trays, leaving plenty of room for spreading, and slightly flatten each ball with the back of a wet spoon.

Bake for 12–15 minutes or until golden.

Remove and cool on the tray or transfer to a wire rack, then serve. The biscuits will keep in an airtight container for up to 1 week.

*Pictured on page 218.*

# AMANDA KELLER'S JAM DROPS

I once made these with Amanda Keller after she rescued the recipe from her mum's repertoire. Amanda was struggling to get it right so we broke it down and adjusted some of the old quantities. We kept the soul and childhood significance, and turned it into a new-age jam drop. Amanda was delighted. I took about twenty home for the kids, but by the time I got there I'd eaten them all!

So what did we learn? Respect the fridge times so that they cook at the right temperature, and keep the jam red: raspberry, plum or strawberry.

125 g unsalted butter, softened
170 g (¾ cup) caster sugar
1 egg
1 egg yolk
300 g (2 cups) self-raising flour,
   plus extra for dusting
pinch of salt flakes
strawberry jam, for piping

**MAKES ABOUT 40**

In a stand mixer fitted with the whisk attachment, cream the butter and sugar for 3–5 minutes until the sugar has completely dissolved and the mixture is pale and creamy. Add the egg and egg yolk and gently whisk until combined.

Scoop the batter into a bowl. Sift over the flour, add the salt and gently fold in with a spatula until just combined.

Line two large baking trays with baking paper.

Roll 2 teaspoons of the mixture into balls slightly larger than a 50 cent piece and place on the prepared trays, leaving a little space for spreading. Using your finger, gently press each ball in the centre to make an indentation. Place the trays in the fridge for 20 minutes.

Preheat the oven to 190°C (fan-forced).

Meanwhile, spoon the jam into a piping bag fitted with a plain nozzle and chill in the fridge for 10 minutes.

Pipe a small amount of jam into the indentation of each biscuit, then bake for 15 minutes or until lightly golden. Remove and cool completely on the trays or wire rack before serving. The jam drops will keep in an airtight container for up to 1 week.

*Pictured on page 219.*

# ROASTED CARROT CAKE

I baked this cake for a CWA competition filmed by *The Living Room*. I tried so hard to tweak the recipe and include different techniques, but I didn't follow the guidelines so I was disqualified! It was the best day competing against the toughest challengers.

Carrot is a naturally sweet vegetable, and when you roast it, it develops marvellous sugars. I like to get fancy with the ribbons to do something different with the presentation, but don't worry if that's not your thing. Just ice it and eat it. The poppy seeds aren't traditional either, but I think they work really well. This is perfect with an afternoon cup of tea.

2 carrots (about 250 g), trimmed, chopped into 3 cm pieces, tops reserved for garnish, plus 1 carrot extra, grated
2 tablespoons vegetable oil
75 g unsalted butter, softened
125 g (⅔ cup) brown sugar
4 eggs, at room temperature, separated
100 g (1 cup) pecans, toasted
225 g (1½ cups) plain flour
2 teaspoons baking powder
1 teaspoon mixed spice
1 tablespoons poppy seeds

**CREAM CHEESE ICING**
250 g cream cheese, softened
100 g unsalted butter, cut into cubes, softened
finely grated zest of 1 lemon
125 g (1 cup) pure icing sugar, sifted
juice of 1 lemon

**SERVES 6-8**

Preheat the oven to 200°C (fan-forced) and line a 20 cm springform tin with baking paper.

Toss the chopped carrots in the oil, spread out on a baking tray and roast for 40 minutes or until cooked through and blistered. Remove and reduce the oven temperature to to 160°C (fan-forced).

Scrape the roasted carrots and oil from the tray into a blender and allow to cool for a few minutes, then add the butter, brown sugar and egg yolks and blend to a smooth paste. Add the pecans and blitz briefly, keeping the nuts in rough chunks.

In a separate bowl, combine the flour, baking powder and mixed spice. Fold in the carrot paste to form a smooth batter.

In a separate bowl, whisk the egg whites until soft peaks form.

Fold the grated carrot through the batter, then add the egg whites, folding in gently to keep the air in the mixture.

Pour the batter into the prepared tin and smooth the surface. Gently tap on the bench to remove any large air bubbles. Bake for 50–60 minutes or until a skewer inserted in the centre comes out clean. Remove and cool completely in the tin.

To make the icing, beat together all the ingredients until light and fluffy.

Carefully remove the cooled cake from the tin and peel away the baking paper. Turn the cake upside-down and ice the top and sides. Garnish with the reserved carrot tops and sprinkle with poppy seeds. The cake will keep in an airtight container for up to 1 week.

**TIP**

If you would like to make colourful carrot ribbons to decorate the cake, peel heirloom carrots into thin ribbons and poach them in a simple sugar syrup (equal parts water and sugar) for 5 minutes. Allow to cool in the syrup, then drain and arrange on top of the cake before serving.

# BLUEBERRY & WHITE CHOCOLATE SCONES

You have to be careful when you speak about scones as people fall firmly into Team Jam First or Team Cream First (my colleague Amanda Keller is Team Cream First). Whichever team you're on, this recipe will please everyone. Another contentious issue is whether you are allowed to use a knife to cut a scone. I vote no.

450 g (3 cups) self-raising flour, plus extra for dusting
¾ teaspoon baking powder
pinch of salt flakes
375 ml (1½ cups) thickened cream
1 tablespoon pure icing sugar
1 vanilla bean, split and seeds scraped
65 g blueberries
3 tablespoons white chocolate chips, frozen
milk, for brushing
jam and extra cream, to serve

**MAKES ABOUT 30**

Preheat the oven to 180°C (fan-forced) and line a large baking tray with baking paper.

Mix together the flour, baking powder and salt in a large bowl.

In a separate bowl, beat together the cream, icing sugar and vanilla seeds.

Take a flat-bladed knife and fold the cream mixture into the dry ingredients using a cutting action until it starts to come together. Turn out onto a floured surface, sprinkle with the blueberries and chocolate chips, and then gently knead to combine, being careful not to overwork the dough. Light scones require a light touch.

Shape the dough into a rectangle about 3 cm high. Using a 4.5 cm round cutter, cut out the scones, pressing down to cut without rotating. Gently re-roll the scraps to cut out a few more. You should have enough dough to make about 30 small scones.

Place the scones about 2.5 cm apart on the prepared tray and brush the tops with milk. Bake for 20 minutes or until golden and they make a hollow sound when tapped on the base. If you can break a scone in half with your hands, it's ready.

Serve warm with jam and cream.

## VARIATION

For an easy cheat's version, combine 300 g (2 cups) sifted self-raising flour, 60 g caster sugar, 1 tablespoon grated frozen unsalted butter and ½ teaspoon salt flakes in a large bowl. Add 125 ml (½ cup) thickened cream and 125 ml (½ cup) lemonade and mix to form a soft dough, being careful not to overwork it. Knead lightly on a floured bench, then gently press the dough with your hands to a thickness of about 3 cm. Use a 6 cm round cutter to cut out eight scones. Place on a baking tray lined with baking paper, then brush the tops with 1 egg yolk mixed with 2 tablespoons milk. Bake in a preheated 220°C (fan-forced) oven for 15 minutes or until lightly golden, then serve warm with your favourite jam.

# FUDGY CHOCOLATE CAKE
## WITH CHEAT'S MIRROR GLAZE

---

Mirror glaze is one of the scariest techniques to attempt for home bakers, but my version is SO easy and will really give you that wow factor when people come over. There's no gelatine involved and there are no complicated steps or processes. The glucose syrup can be bought at any supermarket; you'll find it next to the hundreds and thousands. Just make sure to pour the glaze over the cake when it still very warm and smooth – don't leave it too long or it will set. This is a traditional American-style cake. The amount of brown sugar it contains gives it that lovely fudgy texture and chewy, caramel flavour.

150 g unsalted butter, softened
200 g dark chocolate (70% cocoa
  solids), chopped
165 g (¾ cup firmly packed)
  brown sugar
3 tablespoons caster sugar,
  plus extra for dusting
3 large eggs
110 g (¾ cup) plain flour
pinch of salt flakes
100 g milk chocolate, chopped
raspberries, to serve
vanilla ice cream, to serve

### MIRROR GLAZE
2 tablespoons pouring cream
200 g dark chocolate (70% cocoa
  solids), chopped
2 tablespoons glucose syrup
40 g unsalted butter

**SERVES 10–12**

Preheat the oven to 180°C (fan-forced). Grease a round 24 cm shallow cake tin with butter and line the base with baking paper.

---

Place the butter and dark chocolate in a heatproof bowl over a saucepan of simmering water (don't let the bowl touch the water). Stir until melted and smooth, then remove from the heat and set aside to cool.

---

Whisk together the sugars and eggs in a medium bowl until slightly lighter in colour. Using a rubber spatula, fold in the cooled chocolate mixture, then the flour and salt, and finally fold in the milk chocolate.

---

Pour the batter into the prepared tin and smooth the surface. Bake for 15 minutes or until a crust forms on top. Remove from the oven and cool for a few minutes before inverting onto a cake plate. Stand for 15 minutes, then make the glaze.

---

For the glaze, place all the ingredients in a small saucepan over low heat, stirring occasionally, until melted, smooth and glossy.

---

Pour enough glaze over the cake to just start spilling over the side when smoothed with the back of a spoon. Pour the remaining glaze into a jug to serve. Decorate the cake with raspberries and serve with vanilla ice cream. The cake will keep in an airtight container for up to 1 week.

# WHOLE ORANGE SYRUP CAKE

When I'm making citrus cakes, I don't like to take the pith. This is the fruit equivalent of nose-to-tail eating as every bit of the orange is used. Skin, pith, flesh, juice – it really tastes like orange! Navel oranges are perfect for this recipe as they have minimal pith and usually no seeds. The weight is important as they vary considerably, depending on the season. Don't worry if the batter curdles a bit in the food processor; keep pulsing and it will come back together.

2 navel oranges (about 220 g
   each), washed (see Tip)
185 g unsalted butter, softened
345 g (1 ½ cups) caster sugar
1 teaspoon vanilla extract
3 eggs
335 g (2 ¼ cups) self-raising flour

**ORANGE SYRUP**
220 g (1 cup) white sugar
juice of 2 navel oranges (you'll
   need about 125 ml/½ cup)

**SERVES 6-8**

Preheat the oven to 160°C (fan-forced). Lightly grease a 22 cm springform tin and line the base with baking paper.

Trim the ends of the oranges, cut them into quarters and remove any seeds and the thick core. Roughly chop, then place, skin and all, in a food processor and pulse until roughly chopped. Add the butter, caster sugar and vanilla and pulse until combined (don't worry if it looks curdled). Add the eggs and pulse again, then scoop into a bowl and fold in the flour until just combined. It's not supposed to be a smooth batter so don't overmix here.

Spoon the batter into the prepared tin and gently smooth the surface. Bake for 55–60 minutes or until a skewer inserted in the centre comes out clean. Cool in the tin for 10 minutes, then remove and place on a wire rack, the right way up.

For the orange syrup, working quickly, combine the sugar and orange juice in a bowl, then spoon over the warm cake. Set aside to crystallise and cool. The cake will keep in an airtight container in the fridge for up to 1 week, but leftovers won't last more than a couple of hours!

Make sure your tin is reasonably new to ensure it is non-stick. You don't want to work hard to make the cake and then have it stick to a grumpy old tin.

CHRISTMAS

# THE ULTIMATE SEAFOOD BARBECUE

In Australia, almost everybody has a barbecue and easy access to every possible variety of fresh or saltwater seafood. This is a great centre-of-the-table dish to impress everyone at Christmas, and a really nice treat for your friends and family. The barbecue needs to be super hot and the seafood needs to be cooked very quickly, and not overcooked. Give a pair of tongs to two or three people to help keep things moving. Try and present it simply like we have here – there's no need to plate it up. Serve with lots of tartare or gribiche sauce (see page 115).

2 x 300 g goldband snapper fillets, skin scored, bones removed, cut into 5 cm thick strips
6 raw tiger prawns, peeled and deveined, butterflied
3 scampi, halved lengthways
150 g pippies
250 g mussels, cleaned and debearded
3 baby squid, cleaned, halved and scored
tentacles of 3 Fremantle octopus, cut into 5 cm lengths
6 scallops on the shell, roe removed
2 lemons, cut into wedges
salt flakes and freshly ground black pepper
finely chopped chives, to serve
tartare sauce or gribiche sauce (see page 115), to serve

## MARINADE
1 head of garlic, cloves peeled and finely chopped
2 bunches of chives, finely chopped
4 cm piece of ginger, peeled and finely grated
2 long red chillies, chopped
125 ml (½ cup) extra-virgin olive oil

**SERVES 6**

Preheat the barbecue hot plate to high.

To make the marinade, combine all the ingredients in a large bowl.

Toss the seafood in the marinade and spread out on the hot barbecue plate. Cook until charred and cooked through. Monitor each ingredient as they will all cook at different times.

Squeeze lemon juice over the cooked seafood, season to taste with salt and pepper, and garnish with a sprinkling of chives.

Arrange the cooked seafood on a platter and serve with tartare or gribiche sauce.

# FOOLPROOF TURKEY ROLL

This is a great recipe for people who are scared of overcooking the turkey at Christmas. Poaching is so much easier – it guarantees moisture and has a nice restaurant-quality look. Make sure you apply a lot of pressure when rolling with the foil and ensure there are no perforations for water to get in. The pressure is key.

This can be served with gravy or cranberry sauce, and any of your favourite vegetables or salad greens. I recommend my whole baked cauliflower (page 62), watermelon salad (page 46), baby gem salad (page 54) or tomato and burrata salad (page 64).

90 g unsalted butter
1 onion, finely sliced
1 chorizo sausage, finely chopped
8 thyme sprigs, torn
8 sage sprigs, torn
1 tablespoon sherry vinegar
150 g cooked couscous
90 g (¾ cup) dried cranberries
60 g pistachios, roughly chopped
30 g fresh breadcrumbs
salt flakes and freshly ground
 black pepper
2 turkey breast fillets

**SERVES 8-10**

Melt 40 g of the butter in a frying pan over high heat, add the onion, chorizo, thyme and sage and cook for 5 minutes or until the onion is caramelised. Deglaze with the sherry vinegar, scraping up any bits caught on the base, then remove from the heat. Transfer the mixture to a bowl, then add the couscous, cranberries, pistachios and breadcrumbs. Season well with salt and pepper and mix until combined. Set aside.

Gently remove the skin from the turkey breasts in one piece and reserve. Remove the turkey 'tenders' and set aside. Butterfly the breasts by slicing them in half horizontally without cutting all the way through. Place each breast between two sheets of plastic wrap and flatten with a meat mallet to an even 5 mm thickness. Trim the edges (reserve the trimmings) to make a uniform rectangle.

Place the trimmings in a food processor and process until finely chopped and sticky. Add to the filling in the bowl and mix with your hands until well combined. Divide the filling in half and spread evenly over each breast. Starting from a long side, roll up the turkey to form a tight roll.

For each turkey roll, tear off a double layer of foil, then cover with a piece of baking paper. Place the reserved skin in the centre and smooth it out to as large a piece as possible (trim the skin to make the shape uniform if necessary). Lay the rolled breast in the centre of the skin and, using the foil, roll up to enclose, twisting the ends to tighten. Wrap again in foil as tightly as you can.

Fill a saucepan large enough to accommodate both turkey rolls with water. Bring to the boil, then reduce the heat to a steady simmer. Lower the rolls into the water and weigh down with an upturned plate. Simmer for 30–35 minutes until just cooked through and firm to the touch. (To test, insert a skewer into the centre for 10 seconds. Remove and place on your lip – the tip of the skewer should be warm.) Remove the rolls from the water and allow to drain for a few minutes before peeling off the foil and paper. (If you are not serving them straight away, place the wrapped rolls in an ice bath for 20 minutes, then refrigerate until needed.)

Preheat a barbecue hot plate to high. Melt the remaining butter until foaming, then add the rolls, turning regularly, until evenly coloured and caramelised. Transfer to a cutting board and thickly slice to serve.

# PORCHETTA

I love pork belly because its high fat content keeps it moist and makes it very hard to overcook. If your barbecue has a rotisserie attachment it will be a game changer; if not, just close the hood of the barbie or use the oven.

1.5 kg pork belly, stored uncovered, skin-side up, in the fridge overnight to dry out the skin
finely grated zest of 2 oranges
finely grated zest of 2 lemons
1 tablespoon fennel seeds
2 tablespoons dried chilli flakes, or to taste
2 garlic cloves, grated
5 rosemary sprigs, leaves picked
1 bunch of thyme, leaves picked
1 bunch of sage, leaves picked
2 large swiss chard or mustard green leaves, torn (or use English spinach or Tuscan kale)
salt flakes and freshly ground black pepper
extra-virgin olive oil, for drizzling

**PUMPKIN WITH POMEGRANATE AND HAZELNUTS**
1 large Japanese pumpkin (1.5 kg), unpeeled, cut into 4 cm thick wedges
salt flakes and freshly ground black pepper
2 tablespoons olive oil
1 tablespoon honey
handful of hazelnuts, lightly toasted and skins removed, roughly chopped
seeds of 1 pomegranate
3 radishes, finely sliced on a mandoline
extra-virgin olive oil, to serve

**CHARRED LEEKS**
1 bunch of baby leeks

**SERVES 4–6**

Preheat the barbecue to high, or preheat the oven to 220°C (fan-forced). Remove the pork belly from the fridge to come to room temperature.

Finely chop the zests, spices, garlic, herbs and greens together to combine. Place the pork belly, meat-side up, on a chopping board and sprinkle over the herb mixture to cover. Season with salt and pepper. Tightly roll up the pork belly to enclose the herb filling and truss at 5 cm intervals with kitchen twine, forming a roll with the skin on the outside. Rub a generous drizzle of olive oil into the skin.

If you are using the barbecue, cook the porchetta over high heat for 20 minutes to get a glassy crackling, using a rotisserie attachment if you have one. Reduce the heat to low and cook for a further 1–1½ hours until a meat thermometer inserted in the centre reads 75°C. (Alternatively, insert a metal skewer for 20 seconds and press to your lip; if it feels hot it's ready.)

If you are using the oven for the porchetta, first heat a splash of oil in a heavy-based flameproof baking tray over high heat and shallow-fry the skin all over until little bubbles start popping in the skin. Drain off the oil, transfer to the oven and bake for 15 minutes, then reduce the temperature to 150°C and cook for a further 2 hours or until the internal temperature is reached or it passes the skewer test (see above).

Remove the porchetta from the heat and rest for 10 minutes.

Meanwhile, prepare the pumpkin with pomegranate and hazelnuts. Season the pumpkin with salt and pepper and drizzle generously with oil. Cook on the barbecue, drizzling with honey as you go, for 10–15 minutes or until soft and caramelised.

If you are using the oven, spread over a lined baking tray, drizzle with honey and roast at 220°C (fan-forced) for 25 minutes or so.

To serve, sprinkle over the hazelnuts, pomegranate seeds and radish and drizzle with extra-virgin olive oil.

For the leeks, grill on the barbecue for 20 minutes or until they begin to char on the outside, turning regularly. Remove and wrap them in baking paper, then place in a plastic bag to steam for at least 10–20 minutes (depending on the size of the leeks) until they are completely softened. Remove the burnt outer skins with your fingers and serve the soft, sweet interior.

Remove the twine from the porchetta, cut into slices and serve with the veggies.

The Perfect Christmas Turkey, see page 240
Honey-glazed Ham, see page 241

# THE PERFECT CHRISTMAS TURKEY

The secret to a nice, moist turkey is using plenty of butter under the skin. Use your fingers to carefully separate the skin from the breasts without tearing it. Try to do the same with the legs as well, rubbing plenty of butter all around the joints. There is no such thing as too much butter! You want to use LOTS of stuffing, too, leaving no room at all in the cavity otherwise it will dry out from the inside.

Buy a good-quality, free-range turkey if you can. A smaller one is better – in fact, I'd always get two small ones rather than one massive one. There will be plenty of delicious meat left over – wrap it and putting it in the fridge as soon as you've finished eating, rather than letting it sit out on the table for hours. Use the leftovers for my chicken soup (page 148) or to make meatballs.

1 x 3 kg turkey, stored uncovered in the fridge overnight to dry out the skin
50 g butter, at room temperature
500 g yellow squash, quartered
1 bunch of dutch carrots, trimmed
1 bunch of spring onions, halved
salt flakes and freshly ground black pepper

**STUFFING**
2 tablespoons olive oil
1 onion, finely sliced
4 garlic cloves, minced
½ bunch of thyme, leaves picked and finely chopped, plus an extra handful of sprigs
½ bunch of sage, leaves picked and finely chopped, plus an extra handful of leaves
3 tablespoons peeled, cooked chestnuts, finely chopped (optional)
50 g (½ cup) walnuts, finely chopped
500 g gourmet pork sausages, skins removed, meat broken into chunks
1 egg
45 g dried breadcrumbs
120 g (1 cup) dried cranberries
salt flakes and freshly ground black pepper

**SERVES 6–8**

Preheat the oven to 200°C (fan-forced).

To make the stuffing, heat the oil in a frying pan over medium heat, add the onion and garlic and cook, stirring, for 4–5 minutes until the onion has softened. Remove from the heat. Add the chopped herbs and nuts, sausage meat, egg, breadcrumbs and cranberries. Season and mix together well with your hands.

Stuff the cavity of the turkey with the stuffing. Tie the legs together or use safety pins to close the cavity.

From the neck end of the turkey, gently run your fingers under the skin to loosen, being careful not to tear it. Push some of the butter under the skin of the breast, then make knife incisions into the legs and wings and add the remaining butter under the skin. Arrange the extra thyme sprigs and sage leaves under the skin for presentation.

Place the turkey in a large roasting tin and season the skin generously with salt and pepper. Roast for 15 minutes until starting to brown, then reduce the temperature to 150°C (fan-forced) and cook for 2¼ hours (45 minutes per kilogram). Check it every 20 minutes and baste with the pan juices to stop it drying out. If the skin is browning too much, cover it loosely with foil.

About 1 hour before the turkey is cooked, add the vegetables to the tin and season with salt and pepper. Return to the oven.

At the end of the cooking time check the turkey is done by inserting a small, sharp knife into the fattest part of the thigh. If the juices run clear and the meat pulls apart easily it's ready. If not, cook for a bit longer and check again. Remove and rest for at least 30 minutes before serving with the roasted vegetables. You can flash the veggies in a hot oven again first if you need to.

*Pictured on page 238.*

# HONEY-GLAZED HAM

I really recommend using a good-quality, free-range ham for this recipe. Free-range hams have a higher fat content, more moisture and better flavour. If price is an issue, go for quality over quantity and choose a smaller two kilogram one.

When it comes to the glaze, you need to give it a lot of love and keep glazing the ham constantly as it cooks to achieve that really shiny look. It's all about that baste, 'bout that baste, no treble. You don't need to stick to this traditional glaze either – try being adventurous with Asian flavours like the sweet chilli variation I've given below. Ham works with everything! In fact, you can make this dish all year round. If you have ten people coming over, cook a ham! Make it Christmas every day.

1 large (4 kg) smoked leg ham,
    skin on (or 2 small 2 kg hams)
cloves, for presentation
90 g (⅓ cup) seeded mustard,
    plus extra to serve
90 g (⅓ cup) dijon mustard,
    plus extra to serve
2 tablespoons hot English mustard,
    plus extra to serve
1½ tablespoons Worcestershire
    sauce
300 g honey
2½ tablespoons chicken stock
80 g (⅓ cup) brown sugar

**SERVES 12–14**

Preheat the oven to 200°C (fan-forced).

Skin and peel the ham, leaving some fat on the leg. Using a sharp knife, score the ham in a criss-cross pattern, then push in one clove at the join of each score. Place the ham leg in a large roasting tin.

Combine the mustards, Worcestershire sauce, honey, chicken stock and brown sugar in a large saucepan over medium heat. Bring to the boil, then reduce the heat and simmer until the glaze has reduced and thickened.

Brush some of the glaze over the ham, then place in the oven and bake for 20 minutes. Brush with more glaze three times as it bakes until the ham is golden and crispy.

Pour the glaze from the roasting tin into a jug and brush over the ham immediately before carving. Serve with a range of mustards.

*Pictured on page 239.*

### GLAZE VARIATION

For a sweet chilli–glazed ham, combine 80 ml (⅓ cup) sweet chilli sauce, 1 lemongrass stalk, white part pounded and finely chopped, 2 tablespoons honey, 1 tablespoon fish sauce, 1 tablespoon soy sauce and the juice of 1 lime in a bowl. Garnish with coriander, basil and mint leaves mixed with 1 chopped red chilli, a drizzle of extra-virgin olive oil and a good handful of crispy fried shallots.

# BEST-EVER PAVLOVA
## WITH CITRUS CUSTARD

I love pavlova because it is a classic recipe with a great story behind it, born from the love of a chef for the Russian prima ballerina, Anna Pavlova. Visually it represents her white tutu, and texturally it is an homage to her strong personality hiding a soft heart inside. I always think about this beautiful story when I'm making it.

This is the perfect base recipe for pavlova. If you follow these steps you will never fail. I hate waste so I always use the leftover egg yolks for a custard to serve with the pavlova. You can top it with whatever fruit or nuts you like – it is a blank canvas.

You should always assemble a pavlova just before serving as it doesn't travel well. Embrace the crunch and eat it all at once!

6 eggs, at room temperature
375 g (1⅔ cups) caster sugar
a few drops of lemon juice
1 tablespoon cornflour, sifted
fresh fruit, to decorate

**CITRUS CUSTARD**
340 ml milk
strips of rind from 1 lemon and the
    juice of ½ lemon
3 egg yolks (reserved from the
    meringue)
115 g (½ cup) caster sugar
25 g cornflour, sifted
15 g unsalted butter, at room
    temperature, cut into small cubes

**CHANTILLY CREAM**
300 ml thickened cream
½ vanilla bean, split and seeds
    scraped
1½ tablespoons icing sugar mixture

**SERVES 6-8**

Preheat the oven to 180°C (don't use the fan) and line a baking tray with baking paper. Use an upturned bowl to draw a 22 cm circle on the paper.

Wipe a metal bowl with cotton wool or a clean cloth to ensure it is scrupulously clean and grease free – this is very important, otherwise the egg whites won't whip properly.

Separate the eggs, reserving the yolks for the custard. Make sure there is no egg yolk in the whites.

Using a stand mixer fitted with the whisk attachment or a hand-held mixer, beat the egg whites on a medium setting until soft peaks form. Gradually add the sugar, beating well between each addition to ensure the sugar has dissolved. Once all the sugar has been incorporated, turn the mixer up to high until the meringue has thickened to ribbon stage – when a spoonful poured back into the bowl sits on the surface like a ribbon.

Reduce the speed to medium, add the lemon juice and sprinkle in the cornflour, then continue to beat until the meringue is thick and glossy. Spoon it onto the prepared tray, keeping it inside the circle, and shape it quickly. Don't mess with it too much as you want to get it in the oven pronto.

Place the tray in the middle of the oven and immediately turn the temperature down to 110°C. Clean the mixer bowl and place in the fridge to cool.

Bake for 1 hour 20 minutes or until the meringue has a hard crust but has not taken on any colour. You may see a little sugar syrup seep out of the bottom, which is fine, but the crust should be firm. Inside, it will be soft and marshmallowy. When it's ready, turn off the oven and leave the pavlova inside with door ajar to cool slowly. Don't open the door fully or the pav will crack.

*Continued overleaf >*

For the citrus custard, combine the milk and lemon rind in a saucepan and bring to a simmer over medium heat. Just before it comes to the boil, turn off the heat and leave to infuse for 5 minutes. Strain, discarding the lemon rind.

Meanwhile, cream the egg yolks and sugar in a bowl until pale and fluffy. Add the warm milk and whisk to combine. Pour the custard back into the saucepan and heat over medium heat, stirring constantly to stop it curdling. Do not let it boil. Once it starts to thicken, sprinkle in the cornflour and continue to stir until thick enough to hold its shape on top of the pavlova. Take the pan off the heat and add the butter, bit by bit, whisking until glossy and well combined. Stir in the lemon juice, then set aside to cool completely.

Once the pavlova has cooled to room temperature, make the chantilly cream. Pour the cream into the cooled mixer bowl and whip to soft peaks. Gradually add the vanilla seeds and icing sugar and beat to firm peaks, being careful not to overwhip.

To assemble, transfer the cold meringue to a cake stand and decorate with custard, chantilly cream and seasonal fruit, or any of your favourite toppings.

# YULE LOG
## (BRAZO GITANO)

This Christmassy dessert is sold in every pastry shop in Spain. To get that lovely shape, you need to roll the cake in the tea towel while it's still warm – don't be scared to use some pressure. Be creative with your toppings, too!

1 tablespoon cocoa powder
90 g plain flour
25 g dark chocolate, grated
25 g white chocolate, grated
3 eggs
115 g (½ cup) caster sugar,
    plus 1 teaspoon extra
1 Flake chocolate bar, broken
    into pieces
100 g hazelnuts, lightly toasted
    and skins removed, crushed
red berries, such as raspberries
    or redcurrants

**FILLING**
100 g white chocolate, chopped
250 ml (1 cup) pouring cream

**GANACHE**
100 g dark chocolate chips
100 ml thickened cream
2 teaspoons extra-virgin olive oil

**SERVES 4–6**

Preheat the oven to 200°C (fan-forced). Grease a 30 cm x 25 cm swiss roll tin and line the base with baking paper, extending it 5 cm over the two long sides.

Sift the cocoa and half the flour into a small bowl. Stir in the grated dark chocolate. Sift the remaining flour into another bowl. Stir in the grated white chocolate.

Place the eggs and sugar in a heatproof bowl over a saucepan of simmering water. Using a hand-held electric mixer, whisk for 8 minutes until pale, fluffy and doubled in volume. Pour evenly into the two flour mixtures and stir to melt the chocolate and combine.

Place alternate spoonfuls of the batter over the base of the prepared tin, then swirl with a knife to create a marbled effect. Bake for 15 minutes or until firm.

Place a damp tea towel on the bench, top with a piece of baking paper and sprinkle with the 1 teaspoon of extra sugar. Immediately turn the cake out of the tin onto the paper and remove the lining paper. Using a serrated knife, trim the short edges, then firmly roll up the cake from a short side, leaving the baking paper inside. Cover with a damp tea towel and leave to cool.

Meanwhile, to make the filling, place the white chocolate in a small heatproof bowl. Heat half the cream in a small saucepan until hot, but not boiling, then pour over the chocolate and stir until melted and smooth. Allow to cool completely.

Beat the remaining cream in a small bowl until firm peaks form. Fold one-quarter of the whipped cream into the white chocolate mixture to loosen, then fold in the remaining cream.

Once cooled, unroll the sponge and spread evenly with the cream filling. Roll up again, using the paper as a guide.

To make the dark chocolate ganache, place the dark chocolate chips in a heatproof bowl, heat the thickened cream in a small saucepan until hot, then pour over the chocolate and stir until melted and smooth. Stir in the oil.

Place the rolled sponge on a serving platter and drizzle the chocolate ganache over the top, letting it dribble down the sides. Decorate with the crumbled Flake bar, crushed hazelnuts and red berries and serve. Refrigerate any leftovers and enjoy the next day.

# MY CHRISTMAS PUDDING

This pudding is best freshly poached on Christmas Day. Any leftovers will keep for as long as your leftover ham (say, two or three days). You can fold crumbled leftover pudding through vanilla ice cream, but honestly, if you make a great Christmas pudding there won't be any leftovers! I recommend visiting a Spanish deli to find some special glace fruits for decoration – it's a real Spanish specialty.

185 g (1 cup) mixed dried fruit
½ teaspoon bicarbonate of soda
185 ml (¾ cup) boiling water,
    plus extra for cooking
185 g (1¼ cups) plain flour
95 g (½ cup) dark brown sugar
3 teaspoons baking powder
1 teaspoon mixed spice
pinch of salt flakes
1 x 250 g packet prepared
    suet mix
80 ml (⅓ cup) milk
80 ml (⅓ cup) Pedro Ximenez
    (Spanish sherry) or extra
    orange juice
115 g (⅓ cup) golden syrup
finely grated zest of 1 small orange,
    plus 80 ml (⅓ cup) orange juice
double cream, to serve

### DECORATION
softened unsalted butter,
    for brushing
6 blanched almonds
100 g mixed glace fruits

**SERVES 6-8**

Place the dried fruit, bicarbonate of soda and boiling water in a medium heatproof bowl. Cover and stand for 15 minutes, then drain, discarding the liquid.

Meanwhile, for the decoration, brush a 2 litre non-stick metal pudding basin (with a lid) with softened butter. Arrange the almonds and mixed glace fruit in the base.

Combine the flour, sugar, baking powder, mixed spice, salt and suet in a large bowl. Make a well in the centre, add the drained fruit, milk, sherry, golden syrup, orange zest and juice and mix well. Carefully spoon into the pudding basin over the decoration and secure the lid.

Place an upturned heatproof saucer in the base of a saucepan large enough to hold the pudding. Place the basin on the saucer, then pour enough boiling water into the pan to come three-quarters of the way up the side of the basin. Bring to a simmer over medium heat, then cover the saucepan and cook, adding more boiling water as necessary, for 2¾ hours or until a skewer inserted in the centre comes out clean.

Remove the basin from the water and set aside for 5 minutes, then invert onto a serving plate. Serve with double cream.

# BERRY TRIFLE

Trifle is the perfect Christmas dessert. It is simple to make, using store-bought sponge and custard (though if you'd like to make your custard from scratch, see my recipe on page 243). Best of all, it can sit in the fridge until ready to serve, meaning you can make it ahead and then relax with your guests.

It's worth investing in a beautiful trifle bowl like the one pictured here, and if you really want to impress, don't skip the step about creating the angled jelly! Feel free to vary the ingredients to make it your own – you can use chocolate or mud cake instead of the standard sponge and mix up the fruit however you like. For me, simple is best. I like strawberries as they have a great shape for presentation, and the supermarket sponges are the perfect size and shape.

You'll need to start this recipe the day before to properly set the jelly.

2 x 85 g packets raspberry
    jelly crystals
1 litre store-bought thick custard
1 round store-bought sponge cake
1 litre thickened cream
2 vanilla beans, split and
    seeds scraped
125 g (1 cup) pure icing sugar
500 g strawberries, half hulled
    and halved, half left whole
raspberries, to serve

## PISTACHIO PRALINE
50 g pistachio kernels
100 g caster sugar

**SERVES 10-12**

Take a trifle bowl approximately 20 cm in diameter. Make the jelly according to the packet instructions and pour into the bowl. I like to rest the bowl on an angle in the fridge (propping up the base with a saucer) so the jelly sets on the diagonal, but this is not essential. Leave to set overnight.

To make the pistachio praline, line a baking tray with baking paper. Spread the pistachios over the paper.

Place the sugar in a saucepan and heat, without stirring, over medium heat until the sugar has dissolved and the caramel is a deep brown colour. Pour the caramel evenly over the pistachios and leave to cool and set hard, then roughly chop into pieces.

Once the jelly is set, pour the custard into the bowl to fill the other diagonal half left by the jelly. Sprinkle some of the pistachio praline over the top.

Cut the sponge cake in half horizontally, making two thinner layers (using a piece of string is a great way to do this evenly). Place one of the layers on top of the custard.

To make the chantilly cream, pour the cream into a large chilled bowl and whip to soft peaks. Gradually add the vanilla seeds and icing sugar and beat to firm peaks, being careful not to overwhip.

Layer half the whipped cream over the sponge cake, then arrange half the strawberries around the bowl, with the cut sides to the glass. The sponge will wedge the strawberries to the side of the glass. Repeat with another layer of cake, whipped cream and strawberry halves.

Decorate with the remaining praline and serve with raspberries on the side. If you want to make this ahead of time, the ungarnished trifle will keep, covered, in the fridge for a couple of days. Garnish with the extra praline just before serving.

# CONVERSION CHARTS

Measuring cups and spoons may vary slightly from one country to another, but the difference is generally not enough to affect a recipe. All cup and spoon measures are level.

One Australian metric measuring cup holds 250 ml (8 fl oz), one Australian tablespoon holds 20 ml (4 teaspoons) and one Australian metric teaspoon holds 5 ml. North America, New Zealand and the UK use a 15 ml (3-teaspoon) tablespoon.

## LENGTH

| METRIC | IMPERIAL |
|--------|----------|
| 3 mm | ⅛ inch |
| 6 mm | ¼ inch |
| 1 cm | ½ inch |
| 2.5 cm | 1 inch |
| 5 cm | 2 inches |
| 18 cm | 7 inches |
| 20 cm | 8 inches |
| 23 cm | 9 inches |
| 25 cm | 10 inches |
| 30 cm | 12 inches |

## LIQUID MEASURES

| ONE AMERICAN PINT | ONE IMPERIAL PINT |
|-------------------|-------------------|
| 500 ml (16 fl oz) | 600 ml (20 fl oz) |

| CUP | METRIC | IMPERIAL |
|-----|--------|----------|
| ⅛ cup | 30 ml | 1 fl oz |
| ¼ cup | 60 ml | 2 fl oz |
| ⅓ cup | 80 ml | 2½ fl oz |
| ½ cup | 125 ml | 4 fl oz |
| ⅔ cup | 160 ml | 5 fl oz |
| ¾ cup | 180 ml | 6 fl oz |
| 1 cup | 250 ml | 8 fl oz |
| 2 cups | 500 ml | 16 fl oz |
| 2¼ cups | 560 ml | 20 fl oz |
| 4 cups | 1 litre | 32 fl oz |

## DRY MEASURES

The most accurate way to measure dry ingredients is to weigh them. However, if using a cup, add the ingredient loosely to the cup and level with a knife; don't compact the ingredient unless the recipe requests 'firmly packed'.

| METRIC | IMPERIAL |
|--------|----------|
| 15 g | ½ oz |
| 30 g | 1 oz |
| 60 g | 2 oz |
| 125 g | 4 oz (¼ lb) |
| 185 g | 6 oz |
| 250 g | 8 oz (½ lb) |
| 375 g | 12 oz (¾ lb) |
| 500 g | 16 oz (1 lb) |
| 1 kg | 32 oz (2 lb) |

## OVEN TEMPERATURES

| CELSIUS | FAHRENHEIT |
|---------|------------|
| 100°C | 200°F |
| 120°C | 250°F |
| 150°C | 300°F |
| 160°C | 325°F |
| 180°C | 350°F |
| 200°C | 400°F |
| 220°C | 425°F |

| CELSIUS | GAS MARK |
|---------|----------|
| 110°C | ¼ |
| 130°C | ½ |
| 140°C | 1 |
| 150°C | 2 |
| 170°C | 3 |
| 180°C | 4 |
| 190°C | 5 |
| 200°C | 6 |
| 220°C | 7 |
| 230°C | 8 |
| 240°C | 9 |
| 250°C | 10 |

# GRACIAS

Thanks to the beautiful team that worked on this amazing project – without a doubt the greatest cookbook published this century!

To **Jeremy Simons**, thank you for thinking outside the box and taking photos so differently. Thank you for your great interpretation of my food and sorry I kept touching your screen with my greasy cooking fingers. What shots!

I am very thankful for the wonderful stylist **Vanessa Austin**, for her great vision and understanding of what I like. Such personalised and superb styling, and always going the extra mile … you are just amazing, the best I've ever worked with.

To the kitchen team, **Peta Dent, Sandy Goh** and **Theressa Klein,** thanks for cooking up a storm and never stopping smiling, even on our longest days. Thanks for all your help getting ingredients and for sharing your kitchen with me.

To my wonderful publisher, **Maria Pequeña,** and editors **Clare Marshall, Rachel Carter** and **Naomi Van Groll,** thank you for spending hours and hours making sense of my English and coordinating this mountain of a book. I couldn't have done it without you.

Thank you to **Kirby Armstrong,** for interpreting my vision through your beautiful design.

Thanks to my amazing manager and great friend **Tracy Gualano,** for supporting me and making sure we could find time for this special project. Thank you for making it happen – I'm actually still pinching myself, it is so surreal.

And thanks to my family, **Sascha, Claudia** and **Morgan,** for being my rocks. Even when I miss the important games or school plays, you always encourage me and remain my biggest fans. I do it all for you.

Where I'm from, they say that a chef is only ever as good as his or her team, and I've got the best team in the business and the best jaffle in the world.

*Miguel*
xx

# INDEX

## A

aioli, My quick  29
ajo  77
Amanda Keller's jam drops  221
**anchovies**  12
    Mama Florentina's Russian salad with
        Spanish omelette  56
Anzac biscuits  220
**apples**
    Lemon, thyme & vanilla apple
        crumble  192
    waldorf salad  158
artichokes: Valencia paella of rabbit, beans
    & rosemary (the Spanish way)  87
**avocado**
    Miso chicken bowl  138
    Popcorn fish tacos with corn salsa  116
    Rice-crusted sardines with avo
        on rye  123

## B

baba ghanoush  172
Baja sauce  116
balsamic dressing  51
Banana Joe loaf  209
**bananas**
    Banana Joe loaf  209
    Banoffee pie  194
banh mi, Steak  38
Banoffee pie  194
barbecue, The ultimate seafood  232
Barbecued garlic chicken with cauliflower
    tabbouleh  150
Barbecued harissa lamb with baba &
    Mediterranean bean salad  172
Barbecued jamon-wrapped king prawns  109
Barbecued yoghurt flatbreads  182
Basque burnt cheesecake  204
batter, tempura  129
Bazza's Symi school prawns with Greek
    salad  121
**beans**
    chicken minestrone  148
    Mediterranean bean salad  172
    Rice-crusted sardines with avo on rye  123
    spring vegetables  115
    Valencia paella of rabbit, beans & rosemary
        (the Spanish way)  87
bearnaise, blender  166
**beef**
    Chorizo & beef empanadillas  100
    Herb-crusted roast beef with Yorkshire
        puddings & brussels sprouts  170–1
    koftas  183
    meatballs  164
    Spanish meat pie with wagyu  94
    Steak banh mi  38
    Steak frites with blender bearnaise  166
**beetroot**
    Beetroot flatbreads with koftas & minty
        yoghurt  183
    Beetroot, zucchini & tomato galette with
        amazing buttery pastry  20

    roasted vegetables  142
    Veggie-packed gozleme  184
    Zoodles, cabbage & sesame salad  50
Beetroot flatbreads with koftas & minty
    yoghurt  183
Beetroot, zucchini & tomato galette with
    amazing buttery pastry  20
Berry trifle  250
Best-ever pavlova with citrus
    custard  243–4
**biscuits**
    Amanda Keller's jam drops  221
    Anzac biscuits  220
    Maggie's shortbread  210
blender bearnaise  166
Bloody Mary oysters  110
Blueberry & white chocolate
    scones  224
bolognese, Meatball  164
**bread**
    Banana Joe loaf  209
    Barbecued yoghurt flatbreads  182
    Beetroot flatbreads with koftas & minty
        yoghurt  183
**broccoli**
    Sticky soy barbecued broccoli with coriander
        pesto  44
    tabbouleh  150
    Veggie-packed gozleme  184
broth, Spanish-style chicken and chorizo  148
brownies, Double choc Americano  216
brussels sprouts with chorizo and almonds  170
**burgers**
    Crispy chicken burgers  136
    Crunchy, crispy mushroom burgers  49
butter, clarified  166
butter, garlic  146
buttermilk dressing  54
butterscotch sauce  203

## C

**cabbage**
    cabbage, cucumber and herb
        salad  129
    coleslaw  160
    Miso chicken bowl  138
    Okonomiyaki with chimichurri  25
    Zoodles, cabbage & sesame salad  50
cabbage, cucumber and herb salad  129
**cakes**
    Basque burnt cheesecake  204
    Double choc Americano brownies  216
    Flourless almond–hazelnut chocolate
        cake  212
    Fudgy chocolate cake with cheat's mirror
        glaze  227
    Roasted carrot cake  222
    Show-stopping strawberry cheesecake  200
    Sticky date pudding  203
    Tarta de Santiago  191
    The ultimate ice cream cake with honeycomb
        & a molten caramel centre  215
    Whole orange syrup cake  228
    Yule log  247

**calamari**
    Paella a la Maestre 2021  70
    Salt & pepper calamari rolls  112
Calasparra rice  13
Caldero Murciano  77
candied walnuts  158
**capsicum**
    Chicken & chorizo paella (the Australian
        way)  82
    chunky romesco sauce  174
    Greek salad  121
    *see also* piquillo peppers
caramel  198
carbonara, My favourite chorizo  85
**carrots**
    coleslaw  160
    Fun guy chicken pie  98
    Mama Florentina's Russian salad with
        Spanish omelette  56
    Mama's chicken soup  148
    Meatball bolognese  164
    Miso chicken bowl  138
    poached carrot ribbons  222
    quick pickled vegetables  38
    Roasted carrot cake  222
    roasted vegetables  142, 240
    Spanish meat pie with wagyu  94
    The only lamb shank pie you'll ever
        need  92
    Veggie-packed gozleme  184
    Zoodles, cabbage & sesame salad  50
**cauliflower**
    tabbouleh  150
    Veggie-packed gozleme  184
    Whole baked cauliflower with sweet potato
        hummus  62
**celery**
    Creamy pea & ham soup  67
    Kingfish ceviche  130
    Mama's chicken soup  148
    Posh chicken, herb & mayo finger
        sandwiches  33
    The crunchiest salad ever with buttermilk
        dressing & pangrattato  54
    waldorf salad  158
ceviche, Kingfish  130
chantilly cream  243
**chard**
    Beetroot, zucchini & tomato galette with
        amazing buttery pastry  20
    Porchetta  237
charred leeks  237
cheat's scones  224
**cheese**
    Basque burnt cheesecake  204
    Corn & zucchini fritters with haloumi  19
    cream cheese icing  222
    Fun guy chicken pie  98
    Mac'n'cheese muffins  34
    My favourite chorizo carbonara  85
    parmesan wafers  64
    pesto  78
    Quinoa & sweet potato salad in a jar  51
    Show-stopping strawberry
        cheesecake  200

The crunchiest salad ever with buttermilk
   dressing & pangrattato 54
Whole baked cauliflower with sweet potato
   hummus 62
World champion pizzas 178
*see also* feta, manchego, ricotta
cheesecake, Basque burnt 204
cheesecake, Show-stopping strawberry 200
cherry tomato and fennel salad 126
**chicken**
   Barbecued garlic chicken with cauliflower
      tabbouleh 150
   Chicken & chorizo ballotine 147
   Chicken & chorizo paella (the Australian
      way) 82
   chicken minestrone 148
   Chinese-style chicken soup 148
   creamy chicken and corn soup 148
   Crispy chicken burgers 136
   Crispy chicken schnitzy with buttery centre
      & perfect mash 146
   Family heirloom Spanish chicken pie 103
   Fun guy chicken pie 98
   Mama's chicken soup 148
   Miso chicken bowl 138
   My Thai green curry from scratch 141
   Posh chicken, herb & mayo finger
      sandwiches 33
   Spanish-style chicken and chorizo broth 148
   Valencia paella of rabbit, beans & rosemary
      (the Spanish way) 87
   Your new go-to roast chicken 142
Chicken & chorizo ballotine 147
Chicken & chorizo paella (the Australian way) 82
chicken minestrone 148
chickpeas: sweet potato hummus 62
chilli prawn pici 78
**chillies**
   Baja sauce 116
   Barbecued jamon-wrapped king prawns 109
   chilli prawn pici 78
   chimichurri 25
   chunky romesco sauce 174
   corn salsa 116
   curry paste 141
   Flamenca eggs 28
   garlic, ginger and chilli marinade 232
   ginger dressing 129
   Hot smoked salmon with horseradish cream
      & homemade lavosh 132
   Kingfish ceviche 130
   meatballs 164
   Mediterranean bean salad 172
   Patatas bravas 61
   Porchetta 237
   romesco coulis 109
   sweet chilli–glazed ham 241
   white bean salad 147
chimichurri 25
Chinese-style chicken soup 148
chips 166
**chocolate**
   Banoffee pie 194
   Blueberry & white chocolate scones 224
   chocolate sauce 198, 215
   Churros con chocolate 198
   Double choc Americano brownies 216
   Flourless almond–hazelnut chocolate cake 212
   Fudgy chocolate cake with cheat's mirror
      glaze 227

ganache 247
mirror glaze 227
Tarta de Santiago 191
The ultimate ice cream cake with honeycomb
   & a molten caramel centre 215
Yule log 247
chocolate sauce 198, 215
**chorizo** 12
   brussels sprouts with chorizo and almonds 170
   Chicken & chorizo ballotine 147
   Chicken & chorizo paella (the Australian
      way) 82
   Chorizo & beef empanadillas 100
   Chorizo sausage rolls 105
   Foolproof turkey roll 234
   meatballs 164
   My favourite chorizo carbonara 85
   Okonomiyaki with chimichurri 25
   Spanish meat pie with wagyu 94
   Spanish-style chicken and chorizo broth 148
   Your new go-to roast chicken 142
Chorizo & beef empanadillas 100
Chorizo sausage rolls 105
chunky romesco sauce 174
Churros con chocolate 198
citrus custard 243
clarified butter 166
Claudia's cinnamon crepes 30
**coconut**
   Anzac biscuits 220
   My Thai green curry from scratch 141
coleslaw 160
coriander pesto 44
**corn**
   Corn & zucchini fritters with haloumi 19
   corn salsa 116
   creamy chicken and corn soup 148
   Easy pork san choy bau 155
   Quinoa & sweet potato salad in a jar 51
   Whole baked cauliflower with sweet potato
      hummus 62
Corn & zucchini fritters with haloumi 19
corn salsa 116
coulis, romesco 109
couscous: Foolproof turkey roll 234
crackers, lavosh 132
cream cheese icing 222
cream, chantilly 243
cream, horseradish 132
Creamiest snapper pie 99
Creamy pea & ham soup 67
crepes, Claudia's cinnamon 30
Crispy chicken burgers 136
Crispy chicken schnitzy with buttery centre &
   perfect mash 146
crispy fried chicken 136
Crispy skinned barramundi with cherry
   tomatoes & fennel 126
Crispy skinned snapper with sauce gribiche 115
Crumbed pork cutlets with minted potato
   salad 163
crumble, Lemon, thyme & vanilla apple 192
Crunchy, crispy mushroom burgers 49
**cucumber**
   cabbage, cucumber and herb salad 129
   Crispy chicken burgers 136
   Greek salad 121
   Miso chicken bowl 138
   quick pickled vegetables 38
   Zoodles, cabbage & sesame salad 50

curry, My Thai green, from scratch 141
curry paste 141
custard, citrus 243

**D**
dates: Sticky date pudding 203
**desserts**
   Banoffee pie 194
   Basque burnt cheesecake 204
   Berry trifle 250
   Best-ever pavlova with citrus custard 243–4
   Churros con chocolate 198
   Lemon, thyme & vanilla apple crumble 192
   My Christmas pudding 248
   Orange flans 199
   Show-stopping strawberry cheesecake 200
   Sticky date pudding 203
   Tarta de Santiago 191
   The ultimate ice cream cake with honeycomb
      & a molten caramel centre 215
   Yule log 247
Double choc Americano brownies 216
dough, gozleme 184
dough, pizza 178
Dr Chris Brown's miso salmon 124
**dressings**
   balsamic dressing 51
   buttermilk dressing 54
   ginger dressing 129
   minty yoghurt dressing 183
   sesame dressing 50

**E**
Easy pork san choy bau 155
edamame *see* beans
**eggplant**
   baba ghanoush 172
   My Thai green curry from scratch 141
**eggs**
   ajo 77
   Basque burnt cheesecake 204
   Best-ever pavlova with citrus
      custard 243–4
   blender bearnaise 166
   Chorizo & beef empanadillas 100
   citrus custard 243
   Corn & zucchini fritters with haloumi 19
   Family heirloom Spanish chicken pie 103
   Five-minute tortilla de patatas 29
   Flamenca eggs 28
   Mama Florentina's Russian salad with
      Spanish omelette 56
   Mama's chicken soup 148
   mayonnaise 56
   Murcian salad classica 43
   My favourite chorizo carbonara 85
   Okonomiyaki with chimichurri 25
   Orange flans 199
   Quinoa & sweet potato salad in a jar 51
   sauce gribiche 115
   Spanish meat pie with wagyu 94
   Spanish omelette 56
   Tarta de Santiago 191
   The crunchiest salad ever with buttermilk
      dressing & pangrattato 54
   Yorkshire puddings 170
empanadillas, Chorizo & beef 100
extra-virgin olive oil 12

## F

Family heirloom Spanish chicken pie 103
**fennel**
  cherry tomato and fennel salad 126
  Perfect pork belly with waldorf salad 158–9
  roasted vegetables 142
**feta**
  Beetroot, zucchini & tomato galette with
    amazing buttery pastry 20
  cherry tomato and fennel salad 126
  Greek salad 121
  Lamb montaditos with chunky romesco
    sauce 174
  Little feta tarts 37
  My famous pumpketta 58
  Okonomiyaki with chimichurri 25
  pastry 37
  Veggie-packed gozleme 184
  Watermelon, feta & mint salad 46
**fish**
  Caldero Murciano 77
  Creamiest snapper pie 99
  Crispy skinned barramundi with cherry
    tomatoes & fennel 126
  Crispy skinned snapper with sauce
    gribiche 115
  Kingfish ceviche 130
  Paella a la Maestre 2021 70
  Popcorn fish tacos with corn salsa 116
  Rice-crusted sardines with avo on rye 123
  The ultimate seafood barbecue 232
  *see also* anchovies, salmon, tuna
Five-minute tortilla de patatas 29
Flamenca eggs 28
flans, Orange 199
**flatbread**
  Barbecued yoghurt flatbreads 182
  Beetroot flatbreads with koftas & minty
    yoghurt 183
Flourless almond–hazelnut chocolate cake 212
Foolproof turkey roll 234
Fresh oysters 110
fritters, Corn & zucchini, with haloumi 19
Fudgy chocolate cake with cheat's mirror glaze 227
Fun guy chicken pie 98

## G

galette, Beetroot, zucchini & tomato, with
  amazing buttery pastry 20
ganache 247
garlic butter 146
garlic marinade 150
garlic, ginger and chilli marinade 232
ginger dressing 129
glaze, mirror 227
gnocchi, Sweet potato, with thyme & pine
  nuts 74
gozleme, Veggie-packed 184
gravy 170
Greek salad 121
grilled lamb 174

## H

Herb-crusted roast beef with Yorkshire
  puddings & brussels sprouts 170–1
Honey-glazed ham 241
horseradish cream 132

Hot smoked salmon with horseradish cream
  & homemade lavosh 132
hummus, sweet potato 62

## I

ice cream cake, The ultimate, with honeycomb &
  a molten caramel centre 215
icing, cream cheese 222

## J

jaffles, Jamon & manchego 22
jam drops, Amanda Keller's 221
**jamon** 12, 109
  Barbecued jamon-wrapped king prawns 109
  Chicken & chorizo ballotine 147
  Jamon & manchego jaffles 22
  Flamenca eggs 28
Jamon & manchego jaffles 22

## K

kale and parsley sauce 100
Kingfish ceviche 130
koftas 183

## L

**lamb**
  Barbecued harissa lamb with baba
    & Mediterranean bean salad 172
  Lamb montaditos with chunky romesco
    sauce 174
  The only lamb shank pie you'll ever need 92
Lamb montaditos with chunky romesco
  sauce 174
lavosh crackers 132
**leeks**
  charred leeks 237
  Creamiest snapper pie 99
  Creamy pea & ham soup 67
  Mama's chicken soup 148
  Meatball bolognese 164
  Spanish meat pie with wagyu 94
  The only lamb shank pie you'll ever need 92
Lemon, thyme & vanilla apple crumble 192
**lemons**
  baba ghanoush 172
  Best-ever pavlova with citrus custard 243–4
  brussels sprouts with chorizo and
    almonds 170
  cherry tomato and fennel salad 126
  chimichurri 25
  citrus custard 243
  cream cheese icing 222
  Creamiest snapper pie 99
  crispy fried chicken 136
  Family heirloom Spanish chicken pie 103
  Hot smoked salmon with horseradish cream
    & homemade lavosh 132
  Kingfish ceviche 130
  Lemon, thyme & vanilla apple crumble 192
  Little feta tarts 37
  mayonnaise 56
  minted potato salad 163
  Paella a la Maestre 2021 70
  Porchetta 237
  Posh chicken, herb & mayo finger
    sandwiches 33

Seared scallops 120
Show-stopping strawberry cheesecake 200
Sticky soy barbecued broccoli with coriander
  pesto 44
sweet potato hummus 62
tabbouleh 150
Tarta de Santiago 191
The ultimate seafood barbecue 232
**limes**
  Baja sauce 116
  Bloody Mary oysters 110
  corn salsa 116
  ginger dressing 129
  Hot smoked salmon with horseradish cream
    & homemade lavosh 132
  Kingfish ceviche 130
  Miso chicken bowl 138
  poached sweet potato 130
  sweet chilli–glazed ham 241
Little feta tarts 37
lobster: Caldero Murciano 77

## M

Mac'n'cheese muffins 34
Maggie's shortbread 210
Mama Florentina's Russian salad with Spanish
  omelette 56
Mama's chicken soup 148
**manchego** 12
  Chorizo sausage rolls 105
  Corn & zucchini fritters with haloumi 19
  Flamenca eggs 28
  Jamon & manchego jaffles 22
  My favourite chorizo carbonara 85
**marinades**
  garlic marinade 150
  garlic, ginger and chilli marinade 232
  miso marinade 138
mashed potato 99
mayo, wasabi–soy 49
mayonnaise 56
Meatball bolognese 164
Mediterranean bean salad 172
My quick aioli 29
minted potato salad 163
minty yoghurt dressing 183
mirror glaze 227
Miso chicken bowl 138
miso marinade 138
muffins, Mac'n'cheese 34
Murcian salad classica 43
**mushrooms**
  Chicken & chorizo ballotine 147
  Crunchy, crispy mushroom burgers 49
  Fun guy chicken pie 98
  meatballs 164
  The only lamb shank pie you'll ever
    need 92
  Your new go-to roast chicken 142
My Christmas pudding 248
My famous pumpketta 58
My favourite chorizo carbonara 85
My Thai green curry from scratch 141

## N

**noodles**
  Easy pork san choy bau 155
  Prawn popcorn lettuce cups 129

**nuts**
  Banana Joe loaf 209
  Banoffee pie 194
  brussels sprouts with chorizo and almonds 170
  cabbage, cucumber and herb salad 129
  candied walnuts 158
  Chorizo sausage rolls 105
  chunky romesco sauce 174
  coriander pesto 44
  crumble 192
  Double choc Americano brownies 216
  Flourless almond–hazelnut chocolate cake 212
  Foolproof turkey roll 234
  My famous pumpketta 58
  pistachio praline 250
  Posh chicken, herb & mayo finger
    sandwiches 33
  pumpkin with pomegranate and hazelnuts 237
  Quinoa & sweet potato salad in a jar 51
  Roasted carrot cake 222
  romesco coulis 109
  Tarta de Santiago 191
  The perfect Christmas turkey 240
  Yule log 247

**O**

Okonomiyaki with chimichurri 25
**olives**
  cherry tomato and fennel salad 126
  Chorizo & beef empanadillas 100
  Greek salad 121
  Mama Florentina's Russian salad with
    Spanish omelette 56
  Mediterranean bean salad 172
  Murcian salad classica 43
  white bean salad 147
omelette, Spanish 56
Orange flans 199
**oranges**
  caramel 198
  My Christmas pudding 248
  Orange flans 199
  Porchetta 237
  Tarta de Santiago 191
  Whole orange syrup cake 228
Oysters three ways 110

**P**

Paella a la Maestre 2021 70
**paella**
  Chicken & chorizo paella (the Australian
    way) 82
  Paella a la Maestre 2021 70
  Paella pans 12
  Valencia paella of rabbit, beans & rosemary
    (the Spanish way) 87
pangrattato 54
paprika 12
parmesan wafers 64
**pasta**
  chilli prawn pici 78
  Mac'n'cheese muffins 34
  Mama's chicken soup 148
  Meatball bolognese 164
  My favourite chorizo carbonara 85
  The PPP: Pici Pasta Pesto 78
pastry 37
pastry, rough puff 20

Patatas bravas 61
pavlova, Best-ever, with citrus custard 243–4
**peas**
  Chicken & chorizo paella (the Australian
    way) 82
  Creamy pea & ham soup 67
  Mama Florentina's Russian salad with
    Spanish omelette 56
  spring vegetables 115
  Valencia paella of rabbit, beans & rosemary
    (the Spanish way) 87
perfect mash 146
Perfect pork belly with waldorf salad 158–9
pesto 78
pesto, coriander 44
pickled vegetables, quick 38
**pies**
  Banoffee pie 194
  Chorizo & beef empanadillas 100
  Creamiest snapper pie 99
  Family heirloom Spanish chicken pie 103
  Fun guy chicken pie 98
  Spanish meat pie with wagyu 94
  The only lamb shank pie you'll ever need 92
**piquillo peppers** 13
  Mama Florentina's Russian salad with
    Spanish omelette 56
  romesco coulis 109
  sofrito 70, 82
pistachio praline 250
pizza dough 178
pizzas, World champion 178
poached carrot ribbons 222
poached sweet potato 130
pomegranate: pumpkin with pomegranate and
  hazelnuts 237
Popcorn fish tacos with corn salsa 116
Porchetta 237
**pork**
  Chorizo sausage rolls 105
  Creamy pea & ham soup 67
  Crumbed pork cutlets with minted potato
    salad 163
  Easy pork san choy bau 155
  Family heirloom Spanish chicken pie 103
  Honey-glazed ham 241
  Mac'n'cheese muffins 34
  minted potato salad 163
  Perfect pork belly with waldorf salad 158–9
  Porchetta 237
  Sticky mustard pork ribs with coleslaw 160
  sweet chilli–glazed ham 241
  The only lamb shank pie you'll ever need 92
  The perfect Christmas turkey 240
  see also chorizo, jamon
Posh chicken, herb & mayo finger sandwiches 33
**potatoes**
  ajo 77
  chips 166
  Five-minute tortilla de patatas 29
  Mama Florentina's Russian salad with
    Spanish omelette 56
  mashed potato 99
  minted potato salad 163
  Patatas bravas 61
  perfect mash 146
  roast potatoes 124
  Spanish omelette 56
praline, pistachio 250
Prawn popcorn lettuce cups 129

**prawns**
  Barbecued jamon-wrapped king prawns 109
  Bazza's Symi school prawns with Greek
    salad 121
  Caldero Murciano 77
  chilli prawn pici 78
  Creamiest snapper pie 99
  Paella a la Maestre 2021 70
  Prawn popcorn lettuce cups 129
  The ultimate seafood barbecue 232
**puddings**
  My Christmas pudding 248
  Sticky date pudding 203
  Yorkshire puddings 170
**pumpkin**
  My famous pumpketta 58
  pumpkin with pomegranate and
    hazelnuts 237
pumpkin with pomegranate and hazelnuts 237

**Q**

quick pickled vegetables 38
Quinoa & sweet potato salad in a jar 51

**R**

rabbit: Valencia paella of rabbit, beans
  & rosemary (the Spanish way) 87
**radishes**
  pumpkin with pomegranate and hazelnuts 237
  quick pickled vegetables 38
rainbow chard see chard
**raspberries**
  Berry trifle 250
  Fudgy chocolate cake with cheat's mirror
    glaze 227
  Yule log 247
**rice**
  Calasparra rice 13
  Caldero Murciano 77
  Chicken & chorizo paella (the Australian
    way) 82
  Miso chicken bowl 138
  My famous pumpketta 58
  Paella a la Maestre 2021 70
  Rice-crusted sardines with avo on rye 123
  Spanish bomba rice 13
  Valencia paella of rabbit, beans & rosemary
    (the Spanish way) 87
Rice-crusted sardines with avo on rye 123
**ricotta**
  Beetroot, zucchini & tomato galette with
    amazing buttery pastry 20
  Little feta tarts 37
roast potatoes 124
Roasted carrot cake 222
roasted vegetables 142, 240
rolls, Salt & pepper calamari 112
**romesco sauce** 13
  chunky romesco sauce 174
  romesco coulis 109
rough puff pastry 20

**S**

saffron 13
**salads**
  cabbage, cucumber and herb salad 129
  cherry tomato and fennel salad 126

coleslaw 160
Greek salad 121
Mama Florentina's Russian salad with
  Spanish omelette 56
Mediterranean bean salad 172
minted potato salad 163
Murcian salad classica 43
Quinoa & sweet potato salad in a jar 51
tabbouleh 150
The crunchiest salad ever with buttermilk
  dressing & pangrattato 54
Tomato & burrata salad with parmesan
  wafers 64
tomato salad 28
waldorf salad 158
Watermelon, feta & mint salad 46
white bean salad 147
Zoodles, cabbage & sesame salad 50
**salmon**
  Dr Chris Brown's miso salmon 124
  Hot smoked salmon with horseradish cream
    & homemade lavosh 132
salsa, corn 116
Salt & pepper calamari rolls 112
san choy bau, Easy pork 155
**sandwiches**
  Lamb montaditos with chunky romesco
    sauce 174
  Posh chicken, herb & mayo finger
    sandwiches 33
  Rice-crusted sardines with avo
    on rye 123
  Salt & pepper calamari rolls 112
  Steak banh mi 38
sauce gribiche 115
**sauces**
  ajo 77
  Baja sauce 116
  blender bearnaise 166
  butterscotch sauce 203
  chimichurri 25
  chocolate sauce 198, 215
  chunky romesco sauce 174
  coriander pesto 44
  gravy 170
  kale and parsley sauce 100
  My quick aioli 29
  romesco coulis 109
  sauce gribiche 115
  sesame sauce 38
  tomato sauce 178
  wasabi–soy mayo 49
sausage rolls, Chorizo 105
**scallops**
  Paella a la Maestre 2021 70
  Seared scallops 120
  The ultimate seafood barbecue 232
scones, Blueberry & white chocolate 224
scones, cheat's 224
**seafood**
  Caldero Murciano 77
  Oysters three ways 110
  Paella a la Maestre 2021 70
  The ultimate seafood barbecue 232
  *see also* calamari, fish, prawns, scallops
Seared scallops 120
sesame dressing 50
sesame sauce 38
shortbread, Maggie's 210
Show-stopping strawberry cheesecake 200

snails: Valencia paella of rabbit, beans
  & rosemary (the Spanish way) 87
sofrito 13, 70, 82
**soups**
  chicken minestrone 148
  Chinese-style chicken soup 148
  creamy chicken and corn soup 148
  Creamy pea & ham soup 67
  Mama's chicken soup 148
Spanish bomba rice 13
Spanish meat pie with wagyu 94
Spanish omelette 56
Spanish-style chicken and chorizo broth 148
**spinach**
  Mac'n'cheese muffins 34
  Veggie-packed gozleme 184
  Whole baked cauliflower with sweet potato
    hummus 62
spring vegetables 115
**squash**
  Little feta tarts 37
  roasted vegetables 240
Steak banh mi 38
Steak frites with blender bearnaise 166
Sticky date pudding 203
Sticky mustard pork ribs with coleslaw 160
Sticky soy barbecued broccoli with coriander
  pesto 44
**strawberries**
  Berry trifle 250
  Show-stopping strawberry cheesecake 200
sweet chilli–glazed ham 241
Sweet potato gnocchi with thyme & pine
  nuts 74
sweet potato hummus 62
**sweet potatoes**
  poached sweet potato 130
  Quinoa & sweet potato salad in a jar 51
  Sweet potato gnocchi with thyme & pine
    nuts 74
  sweet potato hummus 62

## T

tabbouleh 150
tacos, Popcorn fish, with corn salsa 116
tarts, Little feta 37
Tarta de Santiago 191
tempura batter 129
Tempura oysters 110
The crunchiest salad ever with buttermilk
  dressing & pangrattato 54
The only lamb shank pie you'll ever need 92
The perfect Christmas turkey 240
The PPP: Pici Pasta Pesto 78
The ultimate ice cream cake with honeycomb
  & a molten caramel centre 215
The ultimate seafood barbecue 232
Tomato & burrata salad with parmesan wafers 64
tomato salad 28
tomato sauce 178
**tomatoes**
  Beetroot, zucchini & tomato galette with
    amazing buttery pastry 20
  Caldero Murciano 77
  cherry tomato and fennel salad 126
  chicken minestrone 148
  chunky romesco sauce 174
  corn salsa 116
  Fun guy chicken pie 98

Greek salad 121
Jamon & manchego jaffles 22
Little feta tarts 37
Meatball bolognese 164
Murcian salad classica 43
The PPP: Pici Pasta Pesto 78
Patatas bravas 61
sofrito 70, 82
tabbouleh 150
Tomato & burrata salad with parmesan
  wafers 64
tomato salad 28
tomato sauce 178
Valencia paella of rabbit, beans & rosemary
  (the Spanish way) 87
tortilla, Five-minute, de patatas 29
trifle, Berry 250
**tuna**
  Mama Florentina's Russian salad with
    Spanish omelette 56
  Murcian salad classica 43
**turkey**
  Foolproof turkey roll 234
  The perfect Christmas turkey 240

## V

Valencia paella of rabbit, beans & rosemary
  (the Spanish way) 87
Veggie-packed gozleme 184

## W

wafers, parmesan 64
waldorf salad 158
walnuts, candied 158
wasabi–soy mayo 49
Watermelon, feta & mint salad 46
white bean salad 147
Whole baked cauliflower with sweet potato
  hummus 62
Whole orange syrup cake 228
World champion pizzas 178

## Y

Yorkshire puddings 170
Your new go-to roast chicken 142
Yule log 247

## Z

Zoodles, cabbage & sesame salad with kewpie
  dressing 50
**zucchini**
  Beetroot, zucchini & tomato galette with
    amazing buttery pastry 20
  Corn & zucchini fritters with haloumi 19
  Little feta tarts 37
  tabbouleh 150
  Zoodles, cabbage & sesame salad 50

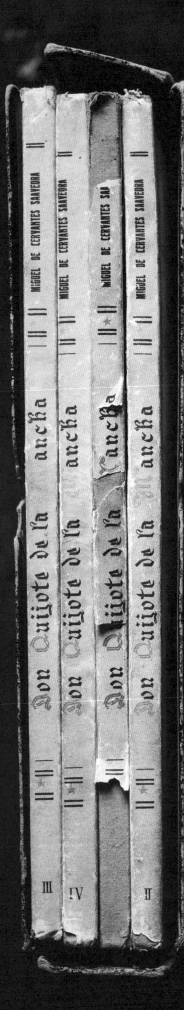

Pan Macmillan acknowledges the Traditional Custodians of Country throughout Australia and their connections to lands, waters and communities. We pay our respect to Elders past and present and extend that respect to all Aboriginal and Torres Strait Islander peoples today. We honour more than sixty thousand years of storytelling, art and culture.

**A Plum book**
First published in 2021 by
Pan Macmillan Australia Pty Limited
Level 25, 1 Market Street,
Sydney, NSW 2000, Australia

Level 3, 112 Wellington Parade,
East Melbourne, VIC 3002, Australia

Text copyright © Miguel Maestre 2021
Photographs Jeremy Simons copyright © Pan Macmillan 2021
Design Kirby Armstrong copyright © Pan Macmillan 2021

The moral right of the author has been asserted.

Design by Kirby Armstrong
Edited by Rachel Carter
Index by Helena Holmgren
Photography by Jeremy Simons
Food and prop styling by Vanessa Austin
Food preparation by Peta Dent, Sandy Goh, Theressa Klein and Miguel Maestre
Typeset by Kirby Armstrong
Colour reproduction by Splitting Image Colour Studio
Printed and bound in China by Hang Tai Printing Co. Ltd.

A CIP catalogue record for this book is available from the National Library of Australia.

10 9 8 7 6 5 4 3 2 1